KEY WEST:

PASSION FOR CUBA'S LIBERTY

HISPANIC AMERICAN COLLECTION # 17

EDICIONES UNIVERSAL, Miami, Florida, 2013

ALEJANDRO F. PASCUAL

KEY WEST:

PASSION FOR CUBA'S LIBERTY

Copyright © 2013 by Alejandro F. Pascual

First Edition, 2013

EDICIONES UNIVERSAL
P.O. Box 450353 (Shenandoah Station)
Miami, FL 33245-0353. USA
Tel: (305) 642-3234   Fax: (305) 642-7978
e-mail: ediciones@ediciones.com
http://www.ediciones.com

Library of Congress Catalog Card No.: 2013
ISBN-10: 1-59388-243-2
ISBN-13: 978-1-59388-243-3

Cover drawing by Sandy Rico.
"The Three Friends Landing Mambises in Cuba"
http://sandyrico-81.wix.com/artwork

Cover Design: Luis García Fresquet

All rights are reserved.
No part of this book may be
reproduced or transmitted in any form
or by any means, electronic or mechanical,
including photocopying, recording or computer systems,
without the written permission of them author, except
in the case of brief quotations embodied in critical
articles or magazines. For information go to
Ediciones Universal.

My gratitude to my friend, Key West artist Sandy Rico for the wonderful cover drawing.

Jose Dolores Poyo y Estenoz

DEDICATED TO:

Jose Dolores Poyo y Estenoz, Havana journalist and patriot who between 1868 and 1903 led the Cuban community of Key West with the highest civic and moral standards devoted to Cuba's liberty.

INDEX

INTRODUCTION		11
I)	CUBA & CAYO HUESO	13
II)	NARCISO LOPEZ	19
III)	A NEW AROMA IN THE CITY	23
IV)	JOSE DOLORES POYO	31
V)	THE SAN CARLOS INSTITUTE	39
VI)	THE STREETS OF CAYO HUESO	45
VII)	JOSE MARTI	57
VIII)	THE WAR OF INDEPENDENCE	71
IX)	REMEMBER THE MAINE	77
X)	AGUSTIN PARLA VS. DOMINGO ROSILLO	85
XI)	AEROMARINE & PAN AMERICAN AIRWAYS	89
XII)	RELATED NOTES	93
	Early Tobacco Briefs	95
	The Loyalty of Freemasons	97
	A Message to Garcia	99
	Juana Borrero, Gloria de Cuba	101
	Mercedes Hospital	105
	Antonio Diaz y Carrasco	107
BIBLIOGRAPHY		109
USEFUL KEY WEST WEB SITES		111

INTRODUCTION

In 1973 I visited Key West for the first time. Nine years before I had left my native enchanted corner of Cuba, Cardenas/Varadero. Key West took me back to my wonderful tropical childhood. I felt at home immediately. The salty air, the lush vegetation, the shady balconies, the endless beautiful sea. That "il dolce far niente" feeling with so many tourists lazily enjoying their day in paradise.

In 2006 our family moved to Key West from New Jersey. We had vacationed here often. We could not wait to be part of the feeling. We knew about the beauty. We knew about the pace. We enjoyed the multicultural flavor. We knew about the role Key West played in Cuba's history. We knew we had black beans, mojitos and cafecito in abundance. But soon we learned, as we settled in town, that this community was also blessed with "angels". There are numerous people who love this community, who give of their time, passion and resources to help many wonderful causes. It reminds me very much of my parents and their friends in Cuba, who before the Castro dictatorship, worked very hard through various civic groups to make our city a prosperous community and a better place to live.

Perhaps inspired by this pleasant surprise, my family and I volunteered to help in the San Carlos Institute in 2007. As we greeted visitors, there were many historical questions asked that we could not answer. Soon I started to look for the history of the Cuban years of Key West from 1868 to 1902. I found very little in the bookstores or the libraries. But consistency paid off as I learned that three individuals who lived in Key West during that era had written numerous works, in Spanish, published in Cuba mostly around the 1930s and 1940s.

One of these writers was Gerardo Castellanos Garcia who was born in Key West. His father, a mid-sized cigar factory owner was one of the most active patriots helping Jose Marti with the preparation of the Cuban War of Independence. They lived on 521 Truman Avenue, where as a child, Gerardo often saw Marti and many of the local community of freedom fighters talk politics and war in his own living room. He even described, in one of his many works, one evening when Marti spoke at the San Carlos. Another jewel is a book entitled "Marti,

Cayo Hueso y Tampa". La Emigracion written by a Methodist Minister named Manuel Deulofeu Lleonard, who lived in Key West for most of those years. In 1905 in Cienfuegos, Cuba, he published his account. Also Fernando Figueredo, General of the Cuban Insurgent Army (Ejército Mambí), who also lived in Key West from 1878 to 1903, left us with several narratives. These works were hard to find. In these pages I would like to share some of the contents of this wonderful treasure.

    I am not a historian, nor a writer, and English is not my first language. The book is written for the locals and visitors who would like to know what happened here in those years. Hopefully after reading these chapters, as you ride your scooter through town, you can dream back about when the aroma of the tobacco leaves permeated our city.

My gratitude to Joe Garrido, Tom Favelli, Alex Vega, Cari Valera, Marlene Carbonell, Marc Cesani, George Lopez, Dr. Glen Westfall and Danilo Salazar for sharing their passion and the information they knew on the subject. Also, to my wife Gloria and children, Michael, Claudia and Giancarlo, who cheered me on. Gloria helped me with translations and my oldest son Michael worked arduously to take the accent away from my written English.

    Many thanks also to my publisher, Juan Manuel Salvat and his team. They are wonderful in any language.

If you would like to send me a comment, please do so at:

afpascual07@aol.com

I

CUBA & CAYO HUESO

CUBA

Christopher Columbus discovered Cuba during his first voyage to the New World in 1492. When Cuba was explored, no sign of any significant amount of gold was found, thus it was left alone as other wealthier lands were exploited of their natural riches. Gold, silver, emeralds, other precious stones, exotic fauna and flora and other valuable items began to be shipped from the Americas to Europe. Taking advantage of the numerous hiding places among the archipelagos throughout the Caribbean, pirates and corsairs began to ambush the galleons which carried the precious cargo.

Spain needed a safe haven where ships could meet on the way to Europe. The site of a wonderful natural bay in the north west coast of Cuba was selected near where the Gulf Stream turns north into the Atlantic and also not far from where favorable easterly winds from Europe approach the Caribbean islands. La Habana was the name given to this perfectly located destination from and to Europe. Its harbor has a small entrance way which opens into three large deep bays. It was founded in 1519. La Habana honors the name of the legendary enchanted daughter of a local Taino chief.

Since the pirates continued their pilferage of the ships sailing east to Europe, it was decided that all ships traveling east bound had to sail into Havana harbor to form convoys that would sail together in large numbers for protection. Havana became the door of Hispanic America. It also became a very important shipyard. Precious woods from around the Havana area were used to repair and make new ships. Since food was needed for the crews while in Cuba and for the journey to Europe, agriculture emerged as an important commodity. With so many goods coming from Europe and many different corners of the Americas trade also developed. As ships went in and out, many interesting characters met in the streets of Havana. It became a fascinating place to live. The city became a splendorous colonial capital with forts, palaces, plazas, distinguished residencies, a cathedral and a large stone wall protecting it all. By the 19th Century sugar, tobacco and coffee were exported in large quantities.

Spanish Galleon

Inspired by the American and French Revolutions, the Freemason movement and by Toussaint L'Ouverture who liberated Haiti in 1797 from French Colonial rule, the Creole classes of Hispanic America began to demand the national freedom of their respective countries. Spain opposed their desire. Nationalist leaders like Simon Bolivar,

Jose de San Martin, Father Hidalgo Costilla and others successfully led the insurrections against Spanish colonial rule in Mexico, Central and South America. By 1850 only Cuba and Puerto Rico remained as Spanish colonies in the Americas.

As Hispanic America fell to the freedom movements, many of the classes loyal to Spain sought refuge in Cuba. The island was thriving in industry and commerce. Thus enough work was available for everyone coming in from the rest of the Americas. Cuba was called "La Siempre Fiel Isla de Cuba" by Spain "The Always Faithfull Island of Cuba." Also "La Joya del Caribe", the "Jewel of the Caribbean."

But the Cuban Creoles also wanted their freedom.

CAYO HUESO

In 1513 while exploring the southern coast of Florida, Juan Ponce de Leon came across a large archipelago made up of more than 400 islands and islets.

He named it the Archipelago of the Martyrs (El Archipielago de los Martires). At its south western extreme they found an island with a beach full of bones, as if a battle had taken place and the bodies were abandoned. They named this island Cayo Hueso, Bone Key. In some old Spanish documents it was also called "Cayo de los Huesos". Since they found no potable water and navigation was difficult in the shallow waters with dangerous reefs, they did not pay much attention to it.

Most historians agree that the first settlers around the Keys were the Caloosa Indians. They held the Cuban Taino tribes from moving up from Cuba. They also battled groups from the Florida peninsula from moving down to the Keys.

In 1815 Juan Pablo Salas, a Spanish Army officer, became the first owner of Cayo Hueso. It was given to him in recognition for his outstanding services on behalf of the Spanish Crown by Juan de Estrada, governor of Florida, based in Saint Augustine. In 1821, as Florida was being traded to the U.S. by Spain, he sold it to John W. Simonton for US$2,000. The transaction took place in Havana. Simonton registered it as Key West, the name given by the locals as it evolved from the mispronunciation of Cayo Hueso.

Juan Ponce de Leon discovered Florida and the Keys.

In 1823 the Navy sent Captain David Porter to settle in Key West in order to protect the commercial maritime routes and to eliminate the pirates from the Caribbean. Since then the US Navy has had a constant presence in Key West.

Two other important events in our story are the construction during the Civil War of the various forts around Key West and in 1867 the laying of the first telegraph cable between Havana and Key West.

The first Cubans to live in Key West were a small group of fishermen who lived between the cemetery and the port. They mostly fished for turtles and gathered sponges. Both were sold in trips to Havana or to tradesmen who came to the Key.

The residents of Key West worked as ship wreckers, fishermen, or in the sponge and salt industries. They had a front row view at the first significant attempt to liberate Cuba from Spain's colonial rule when Narciso Lopez came to town in 1850.

Narciso Lopez

II

NARCISO LOPEZ

Narciso Lopez was a Spanish army officer born in Venezuela. He became dissatisfied with the way in which Spain treated those Cubans who wanted their independence. He joined a group of mostly Cuban and Puerto Rican intellectuals who from New York City plotted to liberate both islands, Cuba and Puerto Rico. One day in 1849, sitting in a park in New York City, Narciso and his friend Miguel Teurbe Tolon designed the Cuban flag. Miguel drew it on a piece of paper as Narciso thought it out. Being Freemasons, a triangle and a star were incorporated into the design. Narciso was preparing an invasion to Cuba to take place the following year and he needed a Cuban flag. Miguel went home and asked his wife Emilia to hand sew a flag from such a design. Thus Emilia Teurbe Tolon hand sewed the first Cuban flag in New York City in 1849.

Narciso had many friends in the American government, especially in the southern states. His plan was to liberate Cuba and to annex it to the United States. By early 1850 Narciso and his approximately 500 men were ready to leave for Cuba. Most of these soldiers where Americans from the states of Kentucky, Louisiana and Mississippi. Promises of land and slaves were part of the enticement. These well armed invaders left from the port of New Orleans on their way to the sugar port of Cardenas on the northern coast of Cuba near Matanzas. The merchant ship Creole served as their vessel. The strategy was to surprise the 400 or so Spanish soldiers in Cardenas. Once defeated they would go by rail to Matanzas where over three thousand citizens would join their forces to take over that city and proceed to Havana.

Very early in the morning of May 19, 1850 Narcizo and his men landed in Cardenas. They took the Spanish garrison by surprise. A bloody battle ensued in the center of the city, lasting over three hours. The Spanish troops finally surrendered. Some eight or so soldiers died on each side. Numerous soldiers on both sides were wounded. Narciso appealed to the local population who became somewhat confused seeing an American liberation army headed by a Venezuelan. Very few if any joined him. Narciso also raised the Cuban flag for the first time on Cuban soil atop the government house in the center of the city. To this day the city of Cardenas is known as "La Ciudad Bandera" or "The Flag City".

The Spanish garrison in Cardenas had alerted the Matanzas forces as soon as the battle began. A large number of Spanish soldiers from that city surrounded Cardenas the night of the 19th. The Spanish forces attacked from three sides, leaving the way to the port free. Narciso viewing the overwhelming numbers of Spanish soldiers ordered his troops back to the Creole.

The Pizarro, a gunner from the Spanish Navy stops in Key West as it searches the waters of the Florida Straits for more invaders. While in Key West it alerts the local authorities of the Cardenas invasion. The 500 or so local citizens of Key West are immediately informed of the news. The Pizarro heads back to Cuban waters as the Creole is making a quick exit from Cardenas Bay with the invaders. Somewhere in the Straits, the Pizarro sees the Creole and a high seas pursuit begins. The Creole heads for Key West desperately. Guns, ammunition and other heavy items are thrown overboard to lighten the ship's load. Anything that is good for burning is thrown into the fire of the steamship. The Pizarro is faster than the Creole and the gap decreases. As the Creole sees Key West in the distance, it heads straight for Fort Zachary for protection. The people of Key West become aware of the chase and climb to the rooftops to get a better view.

As the Creole nears the port, the Pizarro considers to shoot. But the visible batteries at Fort Zach and the presence of a US Navy ship persuades the Pizarro to stop. When the citizens of Key West from their rooftops see the troops inside the Creole they begin to wave and cheer. Narciso and his men conduct a somewhat hasty and disorderly landing, promptly organizing into a march a few blocks from the port. They are received as heroes by Key West. The wounded are treated by the locals.

Narciso's army was officially dissolved in Key West. Most of the weapons were surrendered to the US Navy. The Pizarro remained outside Key West until May 23. That same day Narciso left Key West in a postal ship to Savannah. Before departure he gave Joseph Beverly Browne his saber in gratitude for his hospitality while in Key West. Joseph and Narciso had a common friend, Confederate President Jefferson Davis. Most of the soldiers found ships to return them home.

Some of the badly wounded stayed longer. A few stayed permanently and made Key West their home.

In less than a year Narciso would prepare his next invasion of Cuba. In 1851 he stopped in Key West on the way to Cuba to say goodbye to his friends. Once in Cuba he was captured and hung at La Plaza de la Punta park in Havana in front of thousands of onlookers.

The news of his death resulted in acts of vandalism against Spain in New Orleans and Key West. In New Orleans the Spanish consulate was attacked by a mob and in Key West the liquor store of Francisco Cintas, a Spanish citizen on Duval Street was stoned by local Cubans.

Narciso Lopez two brief visits to Key West sparked the feelings which later on would be the passion of Key West, the quest for Cuba's liberty.

Narciso Lopez troops land in Cardenas, 1850

Emilia Teurbe Tolon hand saw the first Cuban flag.

III

A NEW AROMA IN THE CITY

On October 10, 1868, Carlos Manuel de Cespedes declared war against Spain from his La Demajagua farm in eastern Cuba. He allowed his slaves to go free and asked them to join the ranks of the insurgency. Many of the slaves did join. This historical moment in Cuban history is known as the "Grito de Yara" or "Yara Cry." This event marks the beginning of the Ten Year War in Cuba.

Spain reacts to the Yara Cry by incrementing its injustices against the people of Cuba. Numerous Cubans flee abroad, fearful of being apprehended or worse. They depart to various neighboring countries, but mainly to the United States. The cities of New York, New Orleans, and in particular Key West are chosen for their new lives as exiles. The wealthier Cubans mostly went to New York City.

Those Cubans who chose Key West found that one of the main employers was Seidenberg and Company, a tobacco factory owned by German born Samuel Seidenberg. In particular, its cigar brand "La Rosa Española" was a great commercial success. The Cubans, perceiving the ample national and European markets for quality cigars, began to open their own factories. Many families and friends got together and opened their own "chinchales" in their homes. These small cigar factories either sold their own cigars or rolled for a bigger factory.

The first important tobacco factory in Key West was established in 1831 by William H. Wall. This factory employed around 50 workers but only lasted until 1859. A few individuals, mostly Cubans, rolled for local consumption. As fishermen delivered turtle meat and sponges to Havana they would bring back some goods, among them tobacco leaves for these local "tabaqueros" to roll.

In 1867 Mr. Seidenberg opened his factory. Also some well-known Cuban cigar manufacturers moved the production of their already successful labels to Key West. One of them was Vicente Martinez Ibor, a Spaniard who resided in Cuba, but who was being harassed by the Spanish authorities. His label "Principe de Gales" was already very well known worldwide. Also, Eduardo Hidalgo Gato, who later became the largest cigar employer in Key West with 700 employees, moved to Key West in 1874. The tobacco leaves rolled in Key West were shipped from the province of Pinar del Rio in Western Cuba to Key West and later on to Tampa. The imported leaves were of high quality crops from the well-known Vuelta Abajo region, what is known as "tabaco rubio". The cigars made in Key West were considered of the highest world quality. The principal markets were the large cities in the United States and in Europe. Many of the larger Key West manufacturers had marketing offices in New York City where many European buyers visited.

"Gato 1871" and "Principe de Gales" were two of the best known Key West cigar labels.

As the number of cigar factories grew in Key West, the industry developed a related infrastructure in Cuba. In the northwest coast of Cuba, in the province of Pinar del Rio, a large dock was built so that the tobacco leaves could be rapidly shipped to Key West and later on to Tampa. This small town of Dimas, soon after the dock was built, experienced the construction of numerous tobacco houses where the leaves, packed in bundles, could be stored ready to be shipped. The tobacco steamers did not have to wait for the tobacco to arrive from Vuelta Abajo. The precious leaves were already waiting near the dock.

In Key West as well, entrepreneurs began to import leaves to sell to the local cigar factories. Prior to these middle men the factories would bring the leaves directly from Cuba themselves. Most large factories continued to bring their own tobacco from Cuba while many of the smaller factories opted for the local provider. Tobacco "bodegas" or warehouses developed mostly near the port. The large brick building on Wall Street, where today the Meson de Pepe restaurant is located, housed one of the tobacco importers.

The Cuban immigrants to Key West came from all walks of life, but mostly from the middle and working classes. Key West received an instant influx of professionals from medical doctors and lawyers, to bankers and accountants, writers, poets, artists and musicians. Many of the exiles came from Havana. Havana was one of the most elegant, cosmopolitan and sophisticated cities in the world. It must have been quite a show for the inhabitants of Key West to see this parade of personalities landing at the port. Very few of the Cubans spoke English upon arriving. During those times French was the dominant international language and most educated people throughout the world learned it prior to English. Many of the middle class Cubans were Freemasons. Most of the exiles were Catholics but not great practitioners since they were angered by the pro-Spain posture of the Church.

Many of the professionals who arrived worked in various capacities at the cigar factories. Women also were part of the tobacco work force. The factories had various occupations. There was a leaf selector, a leaf cleaner, the rollers, packers, cleaners and maintenance, management and of course, the lector. Some factories had two or three lectors. The lector is a key figure in the factory. A boring lector would be deadly for a factory. On the other hand, a fun lector could enhance production. One of my uncles who lived in Havana always told me the story of a lector at a Romeo & Julieta factory who was so much fun that everyone wanted to work in his factory. Workers would roll and laugh all day long.

A curious aspect of the Cuban community in Key West is that generally they dressed very well. Even though the climate was identical to Cuba you would hardly see anyone in the streets of Key West dressed sloppy or dirty. The opposite was true, some would overdress in jackets and ties to work in the factories. If you are shown two pictures of cigar factories, one in Havana and one in Key West, you could tell by the elegance which one was Key West.

The Cubans were not an immediate asset to the Key because of the language barrier, but they were not a burden either. The Cuban community took care of its poor and those in need. Slowly integration began and it was tremendously helped by the churches, the Freemason lodges and the arts.

Many local residents married Cuban women. But it seems that not that many local women married Cuban men. Definitely there had to be some ethnic distrust, since biased people exists, but overall there was a common peaceful coexistence which slowly developed into a cultural integration for most of the populace. The Americans were not in love with Spain, thus they mostly felt for the Cuban cause. Many local Americans participated in the Cuban secret cells and amply contributed, purchasing war bonds. The only ethnic tension in town, and a minor one, was between the Cubans and the few local Spaniards. Although many of the Spaniards also favored Cuba's freedom. Some of the most avantguard Conchs took advantage of the Cuban presence to learn how to play double-nine dominoes, puff a good blend, wake up with café con leche and sip a sort of rum and lime concussion that decades later became the Daiquiri. There were no Mojitos back then yet. Most of the accounts I have read say there were two cultures in harmony. A modern day sociologist would probably call it "unity in diversity".

The Cuban community of Key West centered around the tobacco industry and thrived in unison seeking the freedom of Cuba. It is important to acknowledge that the Cuban immigration did not cause a labor problem for the local residents. Rather it increased the demand for goods and services paid for by a new developing industry, luckily a clean one with no industrial residue and with a wonderful aroma that permeated the city.

Many of the tobacco factory owners contributed substantially to the Cuban freedom cause. Among them we have to distinguish

Eduardo Hidalgo Gato who possibly was the person who contributed the most financially to the independence of Cuba in a direct and indirect way through his employees. Gato was also a tremendous benefactor to Key West, donating land, money, and even starting the first city trolley which was mule drawn in its beginning. Mr. Gato several times risked his own life by visiting Cuba in secret missions while faking some business purposes. Three other tobacco factory owners who were fully involved in the struggle for Cuba's independence were Gerardo Castellanos, Vicente Martinez Ibor and Teodoro Perez. There were many others as well.

The "chaveta" is the special blade use to cut the tobacco leaves in the cigar factories. All cigar makers have at least one at their table. Many a professional cigar maker had his own "chaveta" that he would bring to work. Supposely, the best "chavetas" during the Key West tobacco years came from a store in Havana called Cuchilleria de Ribis. Often the excuse to buy "chavetas" in Havana was used by the Key West patriots to engage in anti colonial activities such as to deliver secret messages about expeditions to the insurgents inside Cuba. So when the local patriots needed to send a secret message to Cuba, the expression was, "we need someone to go buy "chavetas". Cigar manufacturers Gato, Castellanos and Villamil were three of the most likely volunteers who often went to Havana at the risk of their lives.

When the Sanjon Peace Treaty was signed ending the Ten Year War in 1878, it was a cause for great sadness in the Key. The insurgents had not accomplished their goal of seeing a free Cuba. Spain pledged to stop persecuting dissidents and many Cubans residents of Key West sadly returned to Cuba. However, many others remained in the Key. For many years the Key felt the absence of those who returned to Cuba. The lack of laborers impacted cigar production. But in a few years, as a result of the bad working conditions in Cuba, many of those who left came back with their much needed skills.

When the Ten Year War ended in 1878 the Key also received twenty or so seasoned, high ranking war veterans from the Mambi (Cuban insurgent) army. These veterans were the pride of the community. Some of them were legendary characters with many interesting war stories to tell. Some were physically impaired from war wounds. When parades took place on Duval Street, which was quite often, this group of veterans would parade together with their uniforms and medals and always received a loud applause from the crowds as they walked by.

Prior to 1868, Key West's population consisted of about 5,000 inhabitants but by 1880 had risen to over 15,000 inhabitants mostly due to the Cuban immigration. Key West increasingly started to smell like tobacco, Cuban coffee, and black beans. At one point, Key West had 119 tobacco factories producing over 300 different labels. As mentioned before, the Eduardo Gato factory was the largest with 700 employees. Gato created a small city known as "Gato Ville" where hundreds of identical small wooden homes housed most of his workers. This neighborhood had convenience stores and other amenities. Nowadays, you can visit Louisa Street a block away from Simonton and see a replica of one of the facades of these homes.

The last Eduardo Hidalgo Gato cigar factory can be visited in the corner of Virginia and Simonton.

Gato's last factory, today converted into an office complex, is worth a visit at the corner of Virginia and Simonton Streets. In both the foyers and entrance hall one can see wonderful artwork and other items related to that era and the Gato family. Other tobacco factory owners also built neighborhoods for their workers, such as Pohalsky and Marrero. In the southwest corner of Truman and White, on White next to the gas station, three small tobacco workers' houses remain from the Pohalsky factory which was at that corner.

Key West tobacco workers, in conjunction with the ship wreckers, contributed to make Key West the richest city in the State of Florida and the tenth in the nation. They helped financed the Ten Year War and even more so, the war of Cuban Independence which began in 1895. In addition to the Seidenberg, Ibor and Gato factories we should also mention the factories owned by Francisco Marrero, Cayetano Soria, Thuman, Antonio del Pino, H.R. Kelly, Julius Ellinger, P.Pohalski and Domingo Villamil were also among the largest.

Castellanos in his book *Motivos de Cayo Hueso* wrote "Small Key West was a capitalist center of world attraction due to the delicate elaboration of the aromatic Cuban cigar."

This community had numerous individuals of great intellect and leadership. Above all, it is important to single out Jose Dolores Poyo, who for over thirty years was the patriotic and civic inspiration for the Cubans of Key West.

Some of the information that I have shared with you in this chapter I have borrowed from the book *Key West Cigar City U.S.A.* written by Dr. Roy Glenn Westfall. This magnificent masterpiece can be purchased in Key West, at "The Meson de Pepe" tobacco shop. If you are interested in tobacco history and particularly in Key Wests', I highly recommend its reading.

The Ten Year War in Cuba began with the Yara Cry

IV

JOSE DOLORES POYO Y ESTENOZ

The Cuban exiles of Key West mostly came from the middle and working classes. This community was known for its patriotism, its generosity, its perseverance and its intensity. Many were the leaders who between 1868 and 1902 led this community with enthusiasm. But among all of them, it's important to honor Jose Dolores Poyo y Estenoz who for more than thirty years was the flame igniting the passion of the Cuban community against Spanish colonial rule. Poyo was born in Cuba in 1837. He came to Key West at age 31 in 1868 with his wife Clara and daughters Celia and America. Blanca, the baby in the family was born in Key West in 1869. As per the Key West census of 1870 it seems that a 28 year old brother or cousin named Ebrain Poyo lived with them. Ebrain's occupation in the census appears as "cigar maker."

Jose Dolores Poyo belonged to the early exiles, who came at the beginning of the "Ten Year War." Among this first group of exiles we also have to add the name of Juan Maria Reyes, a friend of Poyo. Both were journalists in Havana. Both were persecuted by the Spanish authorities. Both found jobs in Key West as readers in the two main tobacco factories of the time. Poyo worked in Mr. Ibor's Principe de Gales factory and Reyes in the Samuel Seidenberg factory.

It's important to note that the work of the reader in a cigar factory was a privileged occupation that was well paid and of high prestige. It was also a key occupation to feed the patriotic conscience of the tobacco workers who listened attentively on a daily basis. The normal working hours for a reader were from 11 AM to 3 PM, but it could vary. The readers would begin the morning with the news, and then stories, poetry, soap operas, civic and patriotic speeches were recited during the day. Some readers would even sing. The tobacco workers would not applaud. They would hit the tables with "chavetas" (cigar blades) or other hard objects to show their approval. Reyes' work as a lector was somewhat precarious in comparison with Poyo's. The Ibor factory where Poyo worked was mainly made up of Cuban exiles and it was blessed with the anti-colonial feeling of Mr. Ibor. However, in the Seidenberg factory, many of the workers were from Spain and Mr. Seidenberg was not so enthusiastic about a free Cuba. Most of the Spaniards were from the Canary Islands and had come to Key West prior to the "Ten Year War". But both Poyo and Reyes enjoyed a wonderful reputation for being prestigious journalists and were quite successful in maintaining a high anti-Spain feeling in Key West.

Jose Dolores Poyo portrait by artist Abel Quintero can be seen at the San Carlos Institute.

Poyo was a good friend of Leoncio Prado, son of the Peruvian President. Prado assigned Poyo as Peruvian consul to Key West. This was a way for Peru to help the Cuban cause. Consequently Poyo's home in Bahama street had diplomatic immunity which came in handy for many war related matters such as hiding secret documents. Poyo looked older than he was. He had a dignified, wise older man look. Many people always sought his advice for endless matters.

A very special feeling reigned in the Cuban community of Key West. They felt as if they were the first city in a free Cuba. They were not living under Spanish colonial rule. In Key West they enjoyed the freedom of this great nation. Here they could dream and act, and they dreamt of a free Cuba that would eventually enjoy these same privileges. They thought of Key West almost as an experiment of what a free Cuban community would later be like in a free Cuba. This community also felt a great pride in having helped in the economic growth of Key West. Poyo and Reyes, as leaders of this community and lovers of this feeling, founded various institutions. Reyes started the "Republicano Newspaper" with Poyo's help, who later became its editor. Poyo with the help of Reyes and many others opened the doors of the San Carlos Institute on the 11th of November in 1871. He also founded the Felix Varela No. 64 Masonic Lodge in 1872 with the assistance of Lino Infante. The founders totaled 13 men and the first meeting took place on May 2 of 1872. Both the San Carlos and the Felix Varela Lodge continue to this day as vital entities of our community.

It's important to mention the tremendous growth of the Masonic lodges among the Cuban patriots. Many of the leaders of the Cuban insurgency reached high ranks as Freemasons. Even the Cuban flag carries Masonic symbols. The triangle represents liberty, equality, and fraternity and the five pointed star is a symbol of the five Masonic virtues.

Poyo was also responsible for the creation of "La Orden del Sol." La Orden del Sol was a secret society with the purpose of helping Cuba obtain its independence. It was the main insurgent cell, with more than 50 members. Each member had to organize its own cell or club or secret society. They were all the same. Consequently, more than 60 secret societies or cells were created in Key West. Most of the help of these societies to the Cuban cause consisted in raising funds to buy arms and to finance armed expeditions to Cuba. Some of them were women only societies. Some of these societies were infiltrated by spies who were paid by the Spanish consul of Key West.

Cuban Republic war bond issued in Key West
and signed by Jose Dolores Poyo.

In 1878 Poyo founded the "Yara" newspaper. This newspaper practically became the official organ of the Cuban exiles in the U.S.. Copies even reached Cuba where they were distributed in high secrecy. Yara circulated for over twenty years.

Two very well-known Cuban patriots who fought during the Ten Year War and who eventually sought refuge in Key West were Jose Francisco Lamadriz and Fernando Figueredo Socarras. These two patriots became an immediate asset to Poyo's leadership. This triumvirate maintained the Cuban community of Key West in high spirits and full of passion for the freedom of Cuba. It's important to mention that the Cuban immigrants, as soon as they could, became U.S. citizens and became involved in local politics. Some of them reached high offices like Fernando Figueredo who eventually was elected to the Florida State Senate. By 1873, the Key West residents of Cuban origins were a majority in the city. Thus, the political weight of the community increased as the years went by. In 1876, Carlos Manuel de Cespedes y Cespedes, son of the late Ten Year War leader, was elected as the first Cuban mayor of Key West. We also have read of some Cubans who became municipal judges and federal custom officials.

Bust of Carlos Manuel de Cespedes y Cespedes,
first Cuban mayor of Key West.

Poyo was surrounded in Key West by people of great knowledge, patriotism, great financial resources and willingness to cooperate with an armed effort to liberate Cuba. Poyo, Lamadriz, and Figueredo were essential to the success that Jose Marti had when he came to Key West to organize the War of Independence. In the chapter entitled Jose Marti, you will see why.

When the Spanish American War ended, and Cuba became a free republic, Poyo returned to Havana where he eventually was appointed as Director of the National Archives. He died in Havana on October

26, 1911. Fernando Figueredo, solemnly spoke at his funeral in the Grand Masonic Lodge of Havana. Poyo was able to reach his dream of seeing a free Cuba. Poyo's greatness was always blessed by his modest and quiet personality. But I feel that these wonderful qualities have deprived him of deserved recognition to his years of leadership and dedication to Key West. We don't have a street named after him. We don't have a statue in any public place. All we have in Key West is a beautiful portrait in the San Carlos. Poyo lived in what is today Bahama Street. Back then, it was better known as "el Callejón de Poyo" or "Poyo's Alley." If you stand in the corner of Southard and Bahama you will see that some grateful soul has placed a wooden plaque acknowledging the "Callejón de Poyo" in his honor. I have nothing to do with this sign but I would love to know who did it.

Wooden plaque on Bahama Street honoring its given nickname "El Callejón de Poyo" or "Poyo's Alley", where he lived.

Poyo and Marti became excellent friends of mutual admiration. There is a photo of Marti which is exhibited at the San Carlos which Marti dedicated to Poyo.

"To Jose Dolores Poyo, to his virtue, to his talent, to his eloquence, to his heart, I dedicate this tribute. His brother, Jose Marti, Key West, May 16th, 1893."

Current facade of the San Carlos Institute on Duval Street

V

SAN CARLOS INSTITUTE

The institutions established by the Cuban community of Key West were many, but none has had the longevity, nor the historical impact, nor the passionate encounters as the San Carlos Institute. The San Carlos was the sacred temple of the Cuban Community. There is no other building in or out of Cuba that matches the historical magnitude of events that took place in the San Carlos in pursue of Cuba's freedom.

The San Carlos was founded by Jose Dolores Poyo and Juan Maria Reyes on November 11th, 1871. It was created as an educational, patriotic and civic center. Its name honors Carlos Manuel de Cespedes who in 1868 declared war against Spain and led the Cuban insurgency in the "Ten Year War." The mission of the San Carlos was to maintain and celebrate the highest civic and patriotic principles among the Key West Cubans. Poyo and Reyes had the intellectual and financial collaboration of Don Alejandro Menendez who was the first academic director of the San Carlos. The president of the San Carlos board of directors at the time was Luis Someillan. The school for boys started in 1871, and it was named Carlos Manuel de Cespedes. The first building was a wooden structure near the port on Anne Street, better known during those days as "El Callejon del San Carlos," or "San Carlos Alley". Since its beginning, both Cuban and American teachers were hired. It was the first English-Spanish, bilingual school of Florida. (It's very curious to know that the first bilingual school of Florida started in St. Agustine where courses were taught in Spanish as well as in a local Native American language.) The school for girls began in 1874. They named it Francisco Vicente Aguilera in honor of this patriot. One of the first teachers was Elisa Figueredo, the daughter of the beloved Perucho Figueredo, writer and composer of the Cuban national anthem.

In 1884, a much bigger San Carlos was built on Fleming Street. This wooden structure had various moments of glory. In 1884 it was visited by Maximo Gomez and Antonio Maceo, top leaders of the Cuban insurgency who were plotting to rekindle the war against

Spain. During this first visit they collected over US$5,000. In October of 1885 Maceo returned to Key West alone. Once again the Cubans were asked to gather at the San Carlos to honor the "Bronze Titan", as Maceo was known. The purpose of this second visit by Maceo was to collect more funds for the war. When Maceo was being introduced, someone from the audience, not too much in love with pomp, interrupted and exclaimed "All present love Maceo and know the purpose of his visit." The man goes up to the stage and places on a table his gold watch. Most of all who were present followed his example and go up on stage and leave cash and their valuable jewelry to be later auctioned. Maceo, totally taken aback by this demonstration of affection and support, also places on the table his own golden tie clip.

San Carlos Institute classroom in 1911

Sadly in April of 1886 a fire consumed half of Key West. The only fire engine owned by the city was being repaired in New York. It was a windy day and almost all buildings from Fleming Street west to the port were ravished by the flames. Houses, churches, government buildings, nineteen or so tobacco factories and the San Carlos were lost. It was a hard blow to the city. Supposedly, the fire started in the San Carlos itself or in a cafeteria next to the building. The possibility that it was sabotage has never been dismissed. The Yara newspaper openly accused Spain for this tragedy.

The magnetism of the San Carlos went beyond the building. The community cleaned the land of the burnt building and under the sun and the moon met to celebrate patriotic holidays and meetings. It was not until 1890 that the new and third San Carlos was built in a large parcel on Duval Street where it is still today.

One of the tobacco factories that burnt in 1886 was the Principe de Gales factory owned by Vicente Martinez Ibor. Ibor decided for various reasons to move his business to Tampa, as did a few other tobacco factory owners. Jose Dolores Poyo, being the reader of the Principe de Gales factory also moved to Tampa for a while. With Poyo in Tampa, Martin Herrera took the responsibility of reconstructing the San Carlos. The construction was finalized in 1890. This new San Carlos was a beautiful brick building. The school occupied the second floor. The lower floor had meeting rooms, offices, and a wonderful theater. Herrera and Poyo could not imagine the historical events that would eventually take place in this building. Jose Marti was yet to enter the history of Key West.

The San Carlos was like the holy temple of the Cubans. The soul of the Cubans in Key West was fed by the constant struggle for the liberty of Cuba. The walls of the San Carlos lived the passions of this community fighting for Cuba's freedom. There is an anecdote about a poster asking the community to attend a patriotic event. The poster had the date and the time, but it did not say where the meeting was taking place. It did not need to. Everyone knew that it had to be at the San Carlos. All parades celebrating the Cuban patriotic holidays would end in the theater of the San Carlos. When Fernando Figueredo spoke at Poyo's funeral in Habana in 1911, he referred to the San Carlos saying, "It was the sacred temple, the holy altar in which at all times the patriotism of that holy community of Cubans met."

Geraldo Castellanos in his exquisite work "Motivos de Cayo Hueso" wrote, "The San Carlos was the most popular and loved place in the Key. The house of everyone. People attended the San Carlos with more fervor than believers go to their places of worship. Cuba does not have a club or society that has in its history such profound greatness, tragedy, pain, sacrifice, tears, and that has housed men of such greatness from the Cuban revolutionary movement such as the San Carlos."

Let me share some of the names of the Cuban insurgency leadership who we know visited the San Carlos and spoke from its podium. In addition to the local patriots, such as Poyo, Herrera, Gato, Lamadriz, Figueredo, etc., we also know of Marti, Gomez, Garcia, Aguilera, Crombet, Cisneros Betancourt, Varona, Gonzalo de Quesada, Sanguily, Cespedes Jr. , Panchito Gomez Toro, Fermin Valdez Dominguez, Carlos Rollof, Serafin Sanchez, and "Mayia" Rodriguez, among others. The podium of the San Carlos from which these patriots spoke is exhibited at the Bacardi Museum of Santiago de Cuba.

Two of the saddest days lived in the San Carlos were the funeral of the community patriarch Jose Francisco Lamadriz in February 1892 and when the death of Jose Marti was known in 1895. Possibly the happiest day in the San Carlos was the 20th of May, 1902, when the independence of Cuba was celebrated in unison with the celebrations in Havana. This was the day the Cuban Republic was born.

The cultural life of the San Carlos, with plays, concerts, and recitals, was quite ample, and it was a reflection of the incredible talent that lived in Key West. The talented artist Joaquin Barroso, alumni of the prestigious San Alejandro School of Havana, directed a school of painting at the San Carlos where numerous local children attended.

In the pages of its website, www.institutosancarlos.org, you can read more of its history. Even better will be to visit it on 516 Duval Street in Key West. You can be part of its history by helping in its preservation by joining the Amigos of the San Carlos program which you can do when visiting the website or when visiting in person. The walls of the San Carlos enclose a very special feeling. To many visitors it is an intimate encounter with the temple that led to Cuba's liberty.

The historic podium of the San Carlos is exhibited at the Bacardi Museum of Santiago de Cuba (Reproduced from the book "Ámbito de Martí" of Guillermo de Zéndegui.)

VI

THE STREETS OF CAYO HUESO

The economic infrastructure created by the tobacco industry in Key West during the second half of the 1800's developed the likes of a Cuban city within the Anglo-Saxon Key. Schools, clinics, churches, restaurants, ice cream parlors, social clubs, Masonic lodges were all established. Domino games, cock fighting, parades and Cuban cultural activities became normal sights. Key West became a small Cuban city within the United States. Spanish at one point became the dominant language of the Key. The arrival of the Cubans in Key West beginning in 1868 was massive in comparison with the local population. In a few years the Cubans were the majority of the population in Key West. Since almost all the Cubans worked in the tobacco factories and other jobs related to it, they did not create a labor problem for the locals. On the contrary, the additional consumption of goods by the new immigrants helped the existent population and the local economy.

The relations between the Cubans and the other islanders kept improving as the Cubans learned English. The relationship between Masonic brothers and church attendees, in particular in the Episcopal and Methodist churches, helped to unite the local citizens with the new arrivals. The political participation of the newly arrived Cubans also helped in this aspect. The Cubans became citizens as soon as they could. This allowed them to vote, to become members of political parties, to carry arms, and to participate in a local type of militia in which they received military training. Of course this was very useful for all those who eventually landed in Cuba to fight with the Mambises. Almost all Cubans joined the Republican party, the party of Lincoln. Some people also called it the party of the blacks since most of the African-Americans were also members of this party. Many members of the local black community helped the Cubans in their struggle to free their homeland knowing that abolishing slavery was also part of the goal.

The Cuban community in Key West was organized into revolutionary cells. The main one was "La Orden del Sol", founded by

Poyo. Antonio Maceo and Maximo Gomez, legendary leaders of the "Ten Year War", were honorary members.

General Maximo Gomez

General Antonio Maceo

Each member of "La Orden del Sol" was required to create a secret cell. The purpose of these cells was to gather funds for the war and to organize and participate in civic activities that would help the community in their main goal of liberating Cuba. The wife and daughters of Poyo founded a very important women-only cell and helped other ladies to establish their own. At one point there were 60 active cells in the community. There were also many non-Cuban Key West citizens who participated in these cells. Many of the non-Cuban residents of Key West helped the Cuban cause. During one of Jose Marti's visits in 1892, Poyo asked him to speak one night in English at the San Carlos in order to thank the non-Cuban allies for their help and participation in the Cuban community activities. Among the Cuban favorite local allies were: Jefferson Brown, George Patterson, William Hunt Harris, the honorable judges Bethel and Locke and in the Hebrew community, Louis Fine and the Steimberg Brothers.

Part of the reason for the secrecy of the cells was the presence in Key West of a Spanish consulate whose consul actively sought informers from within the Cuban community in order to inform Havana of any armed invasions or other revolutionary activities.

Newspapers in Key West were essential to maintaining the passion for a free Cuba alive. Among the first important newspapers was "El Republicano", founded by Juan Maria Reyes. Later "El Yara", founded by Poyo became the main voice of the Cuban exiles in the United States. Later, in 1892, when Marti started "Patria" in New York, it also circulated in Key West. When the Cubans arrived, there were two main newspapers in town, "The Key to the Gulf" and "The Tribune". The latter written by Democrats and the former by Republicans. There were many others, and among them one that was bilingual.

One of the most tense moments in the life of the Cuban community of Key West was caused by a war of words between journalist Gonzalo Castanon, editor of "La Voz de Cuba" in Havana, and Juan Maria Reyes from Key West. Castanon was a journalist totally sold to the Spanish colonial authorities in Havana and was a strong supporter of the "Voluntarios", which was an extreme militia devoted to persecuting the enemies of Spain in Cuba. The accounts of what happened between January 29th and 31st of 1870 varies, but the following seems to come close to the events that took place on those days. Castanon and Reyes through their respective newspapers had been going at each other's throats in various editorials. One of Reyes' comments infuriated Castanon to the point that Castanon challenged Reyes to an arms duel. Reyes' response was that it would be a pleasure to face him in a duel. To everyone's surprise Castanon arrives unannounced to Key West with a group of supporters and his medical doctor. They get rooms in the Russell House which was a hotel located at 114 Duval Street, across the street from Reyes' newspaper. Castanon sends a message to Reyes to come to the Russell House to arrange the duel. Reyes goes to the Russell House with three friends to meet Castanon, among them a Cuban exiled named Mateo Orozco. Reyes and his friends enter the lobby of the Russell House where Castanon and his friends are waiting. Castanon, much bigger and younger than Reyes, slaps Reyes on the face with a copy of the newspaper and rubs it in his face. Orozco, angered by Castanon's actions, takes out a gun. Others in the lobby, among them Castanon himself, do likewise and a shoot out takes place. Castanon drops dead with a bullet in his heart, Orozco is wounded and escapes as well as Reyes and all the other locals. This all happened on the 31st of January. Castanon's body was returned to Havana, in the steamer Lavacca, where the Voluntarios give him a solemn burial. There was a tense atmosphere in the Key, as troops from the local barracks were deployed around the city. Orozco hides for a few days before turning himself in. He is absolved by the local judge since he was acting in Reyes' defense. Needless to say, Orozco becomes a local hero. But, the story does not finish here. This incident was a preamble to one of the most criminal chapters in the history of colonial Spain in Cuba. On the 27th of November of 1871, the Voluntarios in Havana put to the firing squad eight Cuban medical students, falsely accusing them of knife carving Castanon's tomb in the Colon Cemetery of Havana. It was a clear message of vengeance directed towards Key West. Instead of destroying the spirit of the Key West community, this criminal incident made them more determined to fight against an enemy that was even more cruel than previously thought.

Medical students savagely executed in Havana
on November 27, 1871.

One of the most lonely occupations in the Key was that of the Spanish consul. Aside from being in charge of customs and immigration details, his principal job was to spy on the community and to report to Havana. The consul tried to hire spies in the cigar factories, and he also tried to infiltrate the secret societies. He would also report on those from other exile communities that would visit Key West. Constantly he would complain to the state and local authorities of the anti-Spanish activities planned by the Cubans in Key West. When one of the most disliked Spanish consuls departed Key West, he was accompanied all the way to the port by part of the community and a marching band sarcastically wishing him, "Bon voyage."

There were a few marching bands in the community. The main one was called the "La Banda Libertad", organized in the San Carlos by Jose Gonzalez Mendoza. It had about 27 members of high musical talent and patriotism. Among them was the Colombian war veteran Rogelio Castillo Izuñiga. This band was the band that would go to the docks to receive and send off visitors. Often it would participate in activities of the non-Cuban community as well. The song that it would play the most was "The Bayamesa" which later became the Cuban National Anthem. Many non-Cubans in the community knew how to sing along in Spanish. Since the community would look for any excuse for a parade, it was rare the week that "La Libertad" didn't march through the streets of the Key. The band was officially dismantled in a special ceremony in Guanabacoa, Cuba in 1899.

A common practice among the Cubans in the Key was to change the name of the streets. Perhaps by doing this they felt more at home. As examples, Duval Street was called "Banderas" (Flags), Simonton was called "Tablas" (Wood), Whitehead was called "Farola " (Lighthouse), Eaton was called "Iglesias" (Churches), Elizabeth was called "Esponjas" (Sponges). Anne Street was called "El Callejon del San Carlos "(San Carlos Alley) and Bahama "El Callejon de Poyo" (Poyo's alley), there were many others.

Fishing was a popular pastime in the community. One of the better fishing spots was the long dock by the port, which was also a favorite spot for couples to sit by the sea. Another spot was by the lighthouse on Whitehead. I have not been able to assert if it was a small beach, a small dock or both in that location. They called the area "El Sombrero" (The Hat) since that is one of the names they gave the lighthouse. Another favorite fishing place was by South Beach in the corner of South and Whitehead. Next to the 90 miles buoy, which was not there at the time, there is a very small, very strong looking house. The Cubans called that little house "La Casita del Cable" or "The cable's little house". Inside that house is where the telegraph cables from Cuba land in Key West since 1867. In English this little house is better known as the "Western Union Cable Hut". In Cuba the cables land in La Playa del Chivo east of Havana near Cojimar. These are the cables that the Western Union schooner maintained for many years since 1939. The Western Union can be visited at the end of Williams Street.

Something curious about Key West was the lack of influence of the Catholic Church. This had a lot to do with the pro-Spain attitude that the Vatican maintained. Also, as a result of the direct attacks to the Key West community by the Archbishop of Havana, Jacinto Martinez. In 1872, Martinez called of "infidels" the catholic worshippers of the Key because they celebrated in church the anniversary of the "Ten Year War." The local father was reprimanded. In "Motivos de Cayo Hueso, its author, Castellanos mentions the following, "Even though the catholic priests were virtuous and benevolent in Key West and not having provoked any altercations with the Protestants, there were very few Cubans that would follow them." The Protestant churches had a very different posture, in particular the Episcopal and the Methodist churches who both had large followings among the Cubans. Two eloquent ministers, one Episcopalian, Juan Bautista Baez, and another a Methodist, Enrique B. Someillan, combined God and Cuba in their Sunday sermons that were well attended by the Cubans. A curious detail is that at the end of the Spanish American War, the Protestant churches also invaded Cuba. Many of the missionaries that were sent were Cubans from Key West and Tampa. A Methodist Episcopalian Seminary was inaugurated in 1901, partially for this purpose. The Ruth Hargrove Seminary was located on the corner of White and United Streets. But the true passion of the Key was not religion. It was the struggle for Cuba's freedom, and its unchallenged temple was the San Carlos. In many Key West homes it was common to see pictures of Gomez and Maceo, and latter on Marti hanging on the walls.

One of the first schools in the Keys was a Catholic school for girls founded in 1869 by the Sisters of the Holy Names of Jesus and Mary from Montreal. It was called "Mary Immaculate". It had 23 students. The Cubans called them the sisters of Rocky Road. The San

Carlos was founded in 1871 as a bilingual school. Later on, other Cuban schools opened their doors. The Ten Year War veteran Emilio Aimerich y Aulet inaugurated "La Enseñanza Objetiva" located at 1317 Duval where nowadays we can find the Alamo Hotel. This was an all-boys school. Also, in 1888, at the corners of Truman and Duval the "Escuela Laica" of Arturo Cunill was founded. Cunill was very active in the Felix Varela Lodge. Jose Marti, during his visits to Key West, enjoyed very much visiting these schools and even teaching and participating in the academic examinations.

Portrait of Martin Herrera exhibited at the San Carlos.

When I think of Jose Marti in Key West, I can see him walking on Duval Street between Truman and South streets. In that area lived many of his friends. At 1220 Duval was the home of Figueredo where Marti almost always slept. His Key West doctor, Eligio Palma, lived near-by on 1208 Duval. At 1123 Duval was the home of his good friend, Teodoro Perez, where nowadays La Te Da is located. The Aimerich school was at 1317 Duval. Gato's factory was practically around the corner on Virginia. A couple of blocks away on Truman was Cunill's school. And a block from Cunill's at the corner of Truman and Whitehead was a hotel owned by Martin Herrera. His good friend Parla, the owner of a toy store lived near South Beach. His son, Agustin was Marti's godson. Agustin Parla went to become a very important figure in Key West and Cuba's aviation. It is known that Figueredo, Marti and Poyo liked to visit the Salon La Brisa. This party and dance hall was located facing South Beach near the corner of Simonton and South. I am sure as they sat on its balcony having refreshments they gazed at the horizon where Cuba is only 90 miles away.

There were various hotels in Key West. It seemed that the Hotel Duval, of Madame Bolio, and the Russell House were the best known. Both were near the port, across the street from each other, at 119 and 114 Duval respectively, near Front Street. Martin Herrera had a very well-known hotel at the corner of Truman and Whitehead called The Monroe Hotel.

Martin Herrera was one of the most charismatic and loved citizen of the Key. He was the open soul of the Key, one of those who gave everything to his fellowmen. He was always in good humor and with very unique and comical expressions. He never had a penny. He was always on the verge of bankruptcy since his hotel and grocery store supported all those who needed help. When a new family arrived to the Key they would find shelter at the Monroe. If they could paid or not was not relevant. His constant enthusiasm and verbiage of old colloquial Cuban expressions made many laugh. The first time that Marti spoke at the San Carlos on the 3rd of January in 1892, all the great leaders of the community took turns in great eloquence welcoming Marti. When it came to Herrera's turn, everyone held their breath to see what he would say. That night he said a phrase that remained for many years in the folkloric history of the Key, "To the Spaniards, we have to cut their tails up to the last ring." Herrera was able to live his final years in a free Cuba. He died in San Juan and

Martinez, Pinar del Rio, the 1st of August, 1922. There is a beautiful portrait at the San Carlos honoring this patriot of great heart and passion.

Of course, Key West also had Cuban restaurants. One of the best known with Spanish and Cuban cuisine was the Victoria at the corners of Duval and Eaton where Sloppy Joe's is nowadays. Its owner was a Spaniard who was actually very anti-colonial. In one of Jose Marti's visits to the city he offered a free dinner in his honor for 30 people. He was known by his last name, Farto. On Front Street there was a very elegant and loved restaurant of mostly French and American cuisine, "The Louvre." At 720 White Street there was a Cuban restaurant owned by Domingo Abelar where the patriots would often meet to conspire. Marti was there quite often. Two other popular restaurants among the Cubans were El Café de Juan and El Polaco.

The steamers Mascotte and Olivetti used to cover the Tampa, Key West, Havana route. One of them would arrive on Mondays, Thursdays and Saturdays. Sometimes they arrived from Havana and sometimes from Tampa. There were other liners with less frequency that would come from New Orleans, Savannah and Jacksonville. The Havana – Key West trip took approximately 12 hours.

The Cuban presence in Key West did not have a perfect happy ending. Labor strikes by Cubans and layoffs of some of the factory owners escalated into a nasty legal battle in 1894. The problem was especially bad in the Seidenberg factory where management went to Cuba to look for Spaniards to replace some of the striking Cubans. The local Spanish consul had a lot to do with this maneuver. But with the help of a young lawyer from Washington D.C., Horacio S. Rubens, who was a friend of Marti, and the backing of Samuel Gompers, president of the American Labor Federation, the conflict ended in favor of the Cuban workers. But it was a hard hit for Key West. Many of the cigar factories moved to Ibor City, Tampa, West Tampa, and Ocala. Eduardo Hidalgo Gato and others remained in Key West. Luckily the Cuban workers, from their new localities, still supported the Cuban War of Independence, which was just around the corner.

The steamer Olivetti which together with the Mascotte covered the Tampa-Key West-Havana route.

VII

JOSE MARTI

Jose Julian Marti Perez was born in Havana on the 28th of January 1853. Since an early age he felt strongly in favor of Cuba's freedom from colonial Spain. His anti-colonial activities took him to prison in Isla de Pinos at age sixteen. He was pardoned and released after almost two years in jail. But the chains he wore would leave scars and discomfort for the rest of his life. He was send to Spain to keep him out of trouble in Cuba. He studied Law and Letters at the University of Saragoza in Spain. He traveled widely in Latin America, distinguishing himself as a poet, journalist and political analyst.

In 1880 he moved to New York, where he was known for his patriotism, his eloquence and his brilliant pen. In 1891 he was already known by the old leaders who participated in the Ten Year War. His eloquence was already legendary among the Cuban exiles. On October 10th, 1891 he spoke in New York City in celebration of the anniversary of the Ten Year War. His speech was greatly acclaimed by the Cuban exile press. As a consequence of such brilliant speech the Ignacio Agramonte Patriotic Front of Tampa invited him as the main speaker for a 27th of November event marking an anniversary of the killing of eight medical students in Havana by the "Voluntarios." This would be Marti's first visit to Florida.

Marti's speeches in Tampa created an uncontainable furor. The audience would try to approach him to hug and kiss him after these speeches. His two speeches on this journey were on the 26th and 27th of November and they became known as "Los Pinos Nuevos" (The New Pines) and "Con Todos y para el Bien de Todos"(With All and for the Good of All). They are among his most celebrated speeches. Francisco M. Gonzalez, who was assigned by the Yara newspaper to cover Marti's speeches, said that sometimes he would get so caught up in the enthusiasm that he would forget to take notes. The Tampa newspapers reported the magnetism caused by Marti's presence and eloquence. Already many Cuban Americans were referring to Marti as the "Maestro" and "El Presidente", among other names that honored his person.

When the Tampa newspaper's reached Key West and the tobacco workers read what happened in Tampa, they asked the top community leaders, Poyo, Lamadriz and Figueredo, to extend Marti an invitation to visit Key West. Marti was only 38 years old. Almost all the old leaders of the insurrection distrusted Marti or were somewhat jealous of this young man who had never shot a gun, but who already had great influence over the Cuban exiles. Lamadriz had known Marti personally since they both had participated in a Calixto Garcia conspiracy years before. But the Key West triumvirate of Poyo, Lamadriz, Figueredo decided to ask a younger group of leaders to extend the invitation to Marti. This group of young patriots was headed by Angel Pelaez, Frank Bolio, Serafin Bello, Guarterio Garcia, among others.

Marti with the group of young Key West Cubans who invited him to his first visit on December 1891.

In November when Marti went to Tampa, he already had a plan as to how to unite and excite the Cuban exiles in a method to liberate Cuba from Spain. Marti wanted each community to present their ideas in the form of a political platform. At that moment, New York, Tampa, and Key West were the three most important Cuban exile centers. In each city, a number of revolutionary cells had been organized. In New York, Marti had provided the contents of "Los Estatutos Revolucionarios." While in Tampa, he practically took by the hand the group that wrote "Las Resoluciones de Tampa."

When Marti received the invitation to visit Key West, he was filled with joy. But he was also afraid that in a community where so many veterans and leaders of the Ten Year War lived that he would not be welcomed. In Key West lived more than 20 high officials of the Ten Year War. Marti was well aware that Key West was also the wealthiest Cuban exile community and also the tenth wealthiest community in the nation. Profits from the 119 cigar factories of Key West had been generously provided to prior liberation campaigns and Marti hoped that his plans would also be supported in this manner. Marti responded to the Key West invitation positively, with much joy. He prepared a group of exiles from New York and Tampa to accompany him in order to present "Los Estatutos Revolucionarios and the Resoluciones." He was planning on doing the same with the cells in Key West during his visit as he did in Tampa and New York. His plan was to meet with the leaders in order to put together a plan that would represent Key West. Once this Key West plan was finished, all three groups would meet to come out with a single plan to represent the entire Cuban exile community.

The steamer Olivetti covered the Tampa-Key West-Habana and Habana- Key West-Tampa routes. Three times a week the steamer would stop at Key West. On the 25th of December in 1891, amongst its passengers on the Tampa-Key West route was Jose Marti and a delegation of patriots. The departure from Tampa had been enthusiastic, with thousands of tampenos wishing farewell at the port. This was the first time Marti would visit the most important center of the Cuban exile community. Marti was suffering from a bad flu and high fever, but his expectations made him forget his illness. Amongst his worries was how he would get along with Jose Dolores Poyo. To obtain Poyo's backing would be the main goal of his visit. Poyo had the respect and admiration of Cuban exiles everywhere. His newspaper "Yara" had created a wonderful moral and civic conscience among the Cuban exiles. Marti was a great admirer of Poyo, even though they had never met. They had exchanged some correspondence, and Marti, referring to a possible visit to Key West once wrote to Poyo, "Send for me and you will see how I have yearned to shake your creative hands."

Late in the afternoon, the Olivetti reaches the port of Key West. From the distance Marti can see the multitude awaiting at the dock. La Libertad marching band is also present. Among the gathering of men, women, and children, you can see many Cuban and American flags. As soon as Marti appears saluting from the upper deck of the Olivetti, the crowd breaks into applause and welcoming cheers. On the dock by the stairs his old friend Francisco Lamadriz and the committee who invited him are waiting. When Lamadriz and Marti face each other they embrace and Marti says "This embrace is to the old revolution," and Lamadriz responds "My embrace is to the new revolution." When they embrace, the crowd breaks into a huge applause and La Libertad leads the way to the Hotel Duval followed by a welcoming crowd of more than 3,000 people. Since Marti was ill, they offered him a horse drawn caleche but he gracefully declined and walked with the crowd.

It is speculated that perhaps Marti was a bit sad when he didn't see Poyo at the dock. But it is also not known if Lamadriz had a welcoming remark from Poyo. Marti was seen by a doctor upon arrival who recommended that he stay in bed until he was better. The main Cuban political and economic figures of the Key visited him while he rested. Marti took advantage of their visit to begin working on his objectives. Among the visitors was Jose Dolores Poyo.

After a few days in bed, feeling much better, Marti went out to the streets to get to know Key West and its people. He visited several cigar factories where he was given the honor of taking over the lector's chair to address the workers. He enjoyed sharing his enthusiasm for Cuba's liberty and the sacrifices that this task would entail. His enigmatic presence and eloquence met with thunderous applause and cheers. The combination of the year-end parties and the presence of Marti made it an unforgettable two weeks in the Key. One of the highlights of his first visit to Key West was his visit to the Eduardo Hidalgo Gato's factory. The factory was decorated as for a carnival in Marti's honor. There were signs welcoming Marti and even a cannon was shot in his honor. It is speculated that it was during this fiesta in Gato's factory that an older lady for the first time referred to Marti by the name "apostle." Gato and Marti were to become great friends. Similar encounters between Marti and the Cuban community took place in many of the cigar factories where Marti was able to engage the crowd. The invitations and the festivities in his honor were overwhelming and lasted throughout those two weeks. Now the community had felt what they had always heard about. Marti's soft charm and magnetic eloquence had penetrated their souls. The city was jubilant hosting its distinguished visitor.

When Marti sat with Poyo, Figueredo and Lamadriz in order to talk about the necessity for a political party in the Key and for such a party to produce a document similar to the ones from New York and Tampa, Marti was shocked when he read the document that already had been prepared by the people of Key West under the "Convencion Cubana de Key West." Marti simply said ,"Everything has been done here." This document had been written in absolute secrecy and was begun in 1889 by these three patriots and other collaborators, such as Teodoro Perez, Emilio Aimerich, Rogelio Castillo and Gerardo Castellanos Leonart. Often they met at Castellano's home where today 521 Truman is located and also in the school of Aimerich, where the Avalon hotel is today, at 1317 Duval. Marti had no idea of the tremendous work already done by the "Convencion Cubana de Key West". They also already had secret cells inside of Cuba and throughout the Caribbean and Central America.

During the last days of the year and the first days of 1892, the group from New York, Tampa, and Key West met frequently. Among Marti's greatest talents was being a great conciliator. He was able to convince these three groups to drop the divisive items in their respective platforms, and with great favoritism of the works from the Key West Convencion, the platform of the "Partido Revoluncionario Cubano" (PRC) were agreed upon. Marti was designated "El Delegado" which was the top leadership position of the new party. The purpose of the PRC was to organize and carry out a final campaign to liberate Cuba.

On the 3rd of January the Cuban citizens of Key West are asked to meet at the San Carlos. Numerous eloquent speakers take the podium prior to Marti. The fact that Marti was invited to take the podium at the San Carlos already showed the respect and acceptance of the community. Marti's speech that evening was the first of many that he would give in 1892, 1893, and 1894 at the San Carlos. Once again the crowd was treated to exquisite oratory that left them filled with joyful patriotism and hopes for a free Cuba.

Wooden rendition of Marti speaking on the San Carlos balcony.

Aside from uniting the exile community and having written the "Bases", as the political platform of the "Partido Revolucionario Cubano" was known, Marti's third important achievement during this first visit was to convince the factory owners and workers to help finance the new war. Many of the factories were in agreement to give one day's salary per month to the PRC. Eventually all cigar factories participated as well as those from Tampa, Ocala, and the few in New York. This economic backing allowed Marti to eventually drop his main occupations in New York and dedicate himself fully to prepare the War of Independence. The following are two of the many written responses that were sent to Marti by the tobacco workers. These two are found in a wonderful compilation of letters directed to Marti published by Luis Garcia Pascual. Both are from the archives of Professor Diana Abad Muñoz[1].

"Dear Delegate of the PRC:
It's a pleasure to communicate that the workers from the Trujillo Benemeli factory are ready to work the extra day in order to designate, those wages, with pleasure, to our cause.

Francisco Carrazco and Manuel Orta
Cayo Hueso, December 2nd, 1892"

"To the Delegate and members of the local PRC Chapter:
Compatriots, those who signed below, the workers of the "De Villamil Factory" respectfully communicate that very soon we will dedicate a day of work a month to the cause of Cuba's Freedom as the other factories in the community are doing.
Respectfully,
Ruffino Rodriguez, Felix Delgado, and Fernando Guerra
Key West, December 1st, 1892"

Tuesday, the 5th of January was another great day for the Cuban community in the San Carlos. A huge farewell party was organized in honor of Marti. There was music, poetry, acting, and eloquent speeches. The thousands of people in attendance couldn't fit inside the San Carlos. The author Gerardo Castellanos Garcia, who was a young boy then, was present that evening and he shares with us that the activities began at 8:30 at night. He didn't get a seat and was hanging from some theater light fixtures:

"The theater was completely decorated with flags and beautiful curtains. Who is who of the Cuban community was present that evening. There were 13 artistic presentations

---

[1] Exhibited on the walls of the San Carlos, there is a sample of an original "receipt of honor" which was given to the tobacco workers when they gave their monthly contribution to the PRC.

prior to Marti being introduced as the main speaker. He stood up, walked to the extreme right of the stage, nothing moved, nothing could be heard. I'm not exaggerating when I say that you could hear hearts beating, and even though in the crowd there were many who had not yet heard him speak before. I remember all this from that spot where I was in danger of falling. Despite the 43 years that have gone by, my voice and my pulse still tremble as I write these words as I remember waiting for Marti to speak. The crowd was paralyzed with fervor. Finally with his left hand folded behind his back, tenderness in his face, covering everyone with his glance, extending softly his right hand, and with a slight fist elevating his index finger, he gently let out a magic Cubanos !"

"Marti spoke. In his comments about the artistic event that had just taken place, he had beautiful, kind phrases for everyone who participated. Next, he spoke about the union that now was formed. He left everyone in awe with the way he referred to, by name, those who he had met during those past two weeks. The paralyzed audience curiously, in order not to miss a word, would not applaud. It would not dare interrupt the flow of words. Only when a pause was somewhat long, then came the applause like a sordid thunder that would last for many minutes."

Lastly that evening, Marti went up to the second floor balcony of the San Carlos, over Duval street, to salute the crowd that was not able to enter.

The next day as Marti waved goodbye to the huge crowd at the docks, he knew he was leaving behind a new Key West. Inside, he could also feel a renewed self, filled with optimism. Both Key West and Marti had bonded souls. The Cubans now had their own messiah. Many Cuban historians argue that these two weeks in Key West, during his first visit, were among the most significant days of his life.

Three months later, on April 10th, the "Partido Revolucionario Cubano" was officially proclaimed in New York City. Simultaneously, the Key West community met at the San Carlos to commemorate the event. A three story building in the corner of Caroline and Whitehead became the PRC's first headquarters. Mr. Gato donated his schooner "Amada Rosalia" to the PRC. It was very useful to the party. It took local patriots to isolated keys for military training and also transported men and weapons to larger ships. After his first visit to Key West, Marti returned at least on six occasions to organize the war effort. He made a great number of friends in the Key. Among them must single out Poyo, Figueredo and the tabaqueros Eduardo Gato and Teodoro Perez. In Marti's following visits to Key West there was a certain routine observed. He was welcomed at the port by more than 5,000 people. Flags, marching bands, children in school uniforms, all would go to the port. The parade from the port would go to Duval Street passing by the San Carlos and stopping at the home of Teodoro Perez. Once there, Marti would go up to the 2nd floor balcony and would address the crowd. The home of Teodoro Perez was better known to the Cubans as "La Terraza de Marti" or Marti's Terrace. Nowadays that building is still standing, modified, at 1123 Duval. The popular restaurant and night club La Te Da is there today. The name La Te Da developed as a shortening of La Terraza de Marti.

Marti's Terrace, nowadays La Te Da on Duval Street.

One of the main problems Marti faced, and one that bothered him much, was that many cells, in their excitement to fight for Cuba, would send expeditions not coordinated through the PRC. This was mostly the result of old leaders of the Ten Year War showing their independence from the PRC. Marti, who always had a move to counter, assigned the highly respected General Maximo Gomez as the military head of the PRC. All war efforts would be under his command. Gomez, who at the time was in his native Dominican Republic, accepted. Despite Gomez assignment, in one of Martis visits to Key West, he learned upon arriving that the Sartori brothers had successfully landed in Cuba. This news bothered him tremendously and more so when he arrived to "La Te Da" where he found a huge sign honoring the Sartoris on the balcony railings right where he would address the crowd. With much diplomacy he wished the Sartoris much success, but reminded the crowd of the need to unify efforts under the PRC. In private he would share how these solo actions caused lives, weapons and funds to be inefficiently diverted from the main war effort.

One of the basic strategies of the Ten Year War, and other smaller uprisings as well as the one being planned by the PRC, was the weakening of the Cuban economy such as burning sugar cane fields. Those who sponsored these maverick expeditions claimed that is was exactly what they were doing, destroying the Cuban economy. More than 40 expeditions left Key West between 1895 and 1898, mostly under PRC orders.

I remember as a kid visiting the farm of an uncle in Amarillas, Matanzas, and listening to the güajiros (farm workers) talk about the wounded troops of Antonio Maceo and also about the legendary Agüero, who used to burn sugar cane fields. One of the best known expeditions that landed in Cuba was led by Carlos Agüero and Rosendo Garcia. They departed from Key West on April 1st, 1884. They traveled to Cuba aboard the Adrian, captained by a Mr. Johnson. Approximately forty armed men landed in Varadero on the 4th of April. From there they penetrated the heart of the province of Matanzas, which grew extensive sugar cane fields. Their aim was to create as much chaos as possible and to harm the economy by burning sugar cane fields. Thousands of Spanish troops were called to encircle them and little by little they were eliminated. Agüero was eventually killed in the fields of Calimete. Garcia was able to escape and eventually was able to reach Key West.

During one of Marti's visits in 1892 an obelisk was inaugurated in the Key West Cemetery where the monument to the Ten Year War martyrs is. Marti was the main speaker. Many Sundays if there was no other activity, the Cuban community would parade to this monument where the leaders would address the crowd. The obelisk and the monument still stand today.

There are many anecdotes about Marti's visits to the Key. One of my favorite is about a family who gave Marti money so that he could buy himself a pair of shoes since his had a hole at the bottom. Marti goes out shopping and comes back with a rifle saying, "this is what we need". An older lady who is no longer with us, in an article published in the local Key West press around 1970 mentioned how while being a student in the San Carlos, Marti visited the school and gave her a kiss on the forehead.

To Marti, Key West was the most important center of the Cuban exile community. In this community he could see the future of a free Cuba. It was a hard-working community of high civic values, where the rights and the importance of women and of all races, religions, and social classes were respected. He dreamed a free Cuba would be just like it.

Marti's first visit to Key West was on December 25th, 1891 to January 6th, 1892. In 1892, he came back on July 7th for two weeks, in October for a week and on November 9th for three weeks. In 1893, he made three visits in the months of May, September, and December. His last visit seems to have been on May 16th, 1894.

Marti spoke in the San Carlos at least nine times. Seven times he spoke in Spanish, and twice in English. The two speeches in English were on November 23rd, 1892, and on May 18th, 1894. During the first one he thanked the Anglo and Jewish community for their backing of the Cuban cause and he explained the conditions in Cuba and what it would mean for the United States to have a free Cuba as a business partner and political ally. In his second speech in 1894, he tried to appease the bad feelings caused by a labor dispute among cigar workers and factory owners. He did this to bring the peace back to a community that he loved, but also to make sure funding for the war was not affected.

Once during a visit to Tampa, Marti was almost poisoned. It was well known that Spain was after his head. During his visits to Key West it was tried to be kept as a secret where he would sleep. During his first visit, Marti stayed at the Hotel Duval. It is known that on one of his visits he stayed in the Hotel Monroe owned by Martin Herrera at the corner of Whitehead and Truman. But it seems that mostly he would sleep in the home of General Fernando Figueredo at 1220 Duval. That house had a room known in the community as Marti's room. Sadly, that house doesn't exist anymore. Marti most likely felt quite safe with Figueredo since he was a seasoned warrior and well-armed.

Marti's last visit to Key West seems to have been on May 16th, 1894. There is a picture in the San Carlos where you can see Marti with Fermin Valdez Dominguez and Panchito Gomez Toro during this last visit. Fermin, his best friend since childhood, had moved to the Key in 1893 where he worked as a medical doctor. Panchito had arrived with Marti, who wanted the old veterans to see how close he was to Panchito's father, the General Maximo Gomez. It was important to Marti to gain the support of these old generals, who had so much support and clout in the Key. Knowing that they all had tremendous respect for Maximo Gomez, Marti the politician, came to visit with Panchito. Panchito was also the godson of General Antonio Maceo.

Many have been the scholars that have honored Marti with their words. Enrique Jose Varona wrote about Marti:

> "Pilgrim through the world with a lira, a pen and a sword. He sung, he spoke, he battled. Everywhere he left part of his fantasy, pieces of his heart, but in any route, through all the paths, his eye was set on the lonely star that symbolizes his deep and perpetual aspiration of home and country. From his poetry you can smell the sad nostalgia of those without land, of those without country. He makes his pen run wild over the paper. His words cascade over the podiums. You can tell what bothers him, what gives him purpose. The distant vision of Cuba calls him and asks him to write for her and to illuminate the consciences and to ignite the hearts. Here is the deep calling of his soul and the perfect unity of his life. Marti the poet, the speaker, the professor, the consular agent, the journalist, the activist, the conspirator, the statistician, and the soldier. But deeply and always he was only Marti, the patriot."

Statue of Jose Marti at Bayview Park, Key West.

Gomez, Maceo and Marti met at La Mejorana to plan the course of action for the War of Independence.

VIII

THE WAR OF INDEPENDENCE

Once the "Bases" of the PRC were approved by the various exile communities, the next step was to inform those inside Cuba. This was a difficult task. Poyo, Figueredo, Gato, Herrera and Perez advised Marti to trust Gerardo Castellanos Lleonart with this assignment. He had many business contacts and relatives in various cities in Cuba. He also owned a cigar factory in Key West. With the excuse of buying supplies for his business and visiting relatives, he could cover most of Cuba, hopefully, not arousing suspicion. Even in the Key it was kept with utmost secrecy. Only the small group mentioned above knew about it. On August 9, 1892 Castellanos departed for Havana. Hiding in his garments were hand written letters, signed by Marti, addressed to key insurgent leaders inside of Cuba. The basic message contained in the letters was about the creation of the PRC, how enough funds were anticipated to buy weapons and ammunitions and asking those inside Cuba to get ready for battle. The order as to when would be the proper time to initiate the war will follow when circumstances fall in place. The message also asked those who received it, to spread the word secretly among supporters.

Castellanos successfully covered most of Cuba and came back with mostly positive feedback. Most Cuban patriots were enthusiastically awaiting Marti's orders to initiate the new war. Castellanos returned twice again to Cuba further organizing the coming uprising.

The war for Cuba's independence finally begins in February of 1895. The secret order to begin the war is sent by Marti from New York to Key West in the hands of Gonzalo de Quesada. Quesada on the way to the Key stops in Tampa and visits the tabaquero Blas Fernandez. Fernandez rolls the secret document inside a cigar. This cigar is placed in a box with the rest of the cigars and the box is sealed. Quesada takes the box to the Key and gives it to Miguel Angel Duque. Duque embarks the Mascotti for Havana. When he reaches Cuba, he takes the box to Juan Gualberto Gomez, head of the PRC in Cuba, who jointly with the other members of the party reads the note and decides that February 24th would be the perfect day to initiate the war, coinciding with carnival festivities.

The secrecy of the operation was a total success. On the morning of February 24, 1895 the patriots rose in three parts of eastern Cuba, in the cities of Baire and Guantanamo and in a farm known as Colmenar de Bayate. Also in the province of Matanzas, a group under Juan Gualberto Gomez rose in Ibarra. The groups in eastern Cuba confronted Spanish troops with success and then penetrated the fields to continue the war. The group in Ibarra was defeated. Some were killed, others were put to the firing squads. Juan Gualberto was lucky that he was only deported to Spain.

Marti and Maximo Gomez landed in Playitas, Cuba on the 12th of April, 1895. Antonio Maceo had already landed and organized his troops some weeks before. On the 5th of May, all three, Maceo, Marti, and Gomez meet in the farm of "La Mejorana". On the 19th of that same month Marti is shot and dies during the Battle of Dos Rios. Two days later on the 21st of May, the following article appears in Havana's main newspaper "El Diario de la Marina."

> *"Important telegram, Jose Marti is dead:" "In the Spanish Army headquarters we have received today this very important telegram which has been sent by General Salcedo from Santiago de Cuba:*
>
> *"Santiago de Cuba, 21st of May,*
> *"Chief General:*
> *"Yesterday in a combat I consider of high political transcendence. Through confidential sources I learned that a sizeable group of insurgents were camping between the Palma and Remanganaguas rivers. I sent Colonel Sandoval with his army which met which such group between Vijas and Dos Rios right corner of the Contramaestre river approximately 700 men with Marti, Gomez, Masso and Borrero. They were heading to cross the Cauto river in the direction of Tunas and Principe. Combat lasted an hour and a half, enemy was taken out of position, escaping in three sub-divided fractions, being pursuit and having been killed, the so called "President" of the Cuban Republic whose body has been recovered and identified despite the enemy trying to recover it. In addition, the*

enemy had at least 14 more dead and many wounded. We have taken many weapons, and Marti's correspondence. Thirty seven horses also dead, and eleven alive with their saddling. We lost five dead, and seven wounded. Prisoners assured that Gomez and Estrada are either dead or wounded. But we have no evidence in this regard. We will try to find out."

Salcedo"

An absolute silence covered the streets of Key West when they learned the news. There was never a sadder day in the Key.

On the 4th of June, three weeks after Marti's death, the New York Times reported that there was a carnival going on in Key West, after a telegram arrived from Santo Domingo, supposedly from Panchito Gomez Toro sharing that Marti was alive. The Cubans gathered at the San Carlos where a great parade erupted in celebration.

From New York, Carmita Mantilla, sister of Maria, Marti's godchild, also a victim of the erroneous news, sent a letter to Marti dated June 6th, 1895 from Central Valley, New York (this letter is also from Ruiz Pascual's compilation):

"My Dearest Marti:
I have seen, with much happiness, your beautiful letters that since you stepped in our beloved Cuba you are like another man, and I understand it.
The Americans here only speak about the Cuban revolution and they love you very much. Mr. Ficken says that you are even better than George Washington in many respects (of course I believe that there is no man in this world that can compare to you), and he's always saying, "I love that man". And he has a lot of desire to meet you. I tell you this just so that you have an idea of the sympathy that the American people have for you and for the revolution. It is the general feeling that there is not an American that is not siding with the Cubans. Soon we are going to have a concert to benefit Cuba. The Central Valley league is preparing a reception in your honor for your arrival. These small details are so that you'll see how much you are loved in the United States.

Tell General Gomez that here we love him very much and that we know that you are both taking care of each other. How much I long to be by your side ! Maria doesn't write to you now because she's in New York helping Uba who should soon come here and visit. With you and Maximo Gomez and a few other good Cubans, we have no doubt you will be victorious.
Always with you,

Carmita Mantilla y Miyares"

For three long years the insurgent troops or "Mambises", fought from the eastern end of Cuba to the western tip. The word Mambi comes from a Dominican patriot named Eutemio Mamby. He was an officer in the Spanish army who defected into the ranks of the Dominican insurgents and taught them how to fight with machetes in hand. Maximo Gomez, who was also Dominican, learned from him and taught the Cubans.

During the Ten Year War in 1868, when the Spanish troops saw the Cubans charging wielding machetes they said "Just like the Mamby soldiers". The word stuck since and was modified to Mambi since in the Spanish language the " y "and the "i" are pronounce exactly alike. Mambises is the plural of Mambi.

In Key West no one would miss a single piece of news coming from the island. The exile population faithfully backed their heroes. Men and weapons were continuously and secretly sent to Cuba. Three ships, in particular, were well-known to the American navy and were often persecuted by the Spanish navy; the Monarch, the Three Friends, and the Dauntless. These three vessels were responsible for more than sixteen successful landings in Cuba. General Emilio Nuñez was in charge of most of these missions. Spain constantly complained to the U.S. government about the revolutionary activities that the Cubans in Key West were involved in.

At one point during the war the expeditions from Key West became crucial. When Maceo and his troops penetrated the Province of Pinar del Rio in the extreme west of Cuba, the Spanish tried to isolate the insurgent troops by creating a security zone that closed Maceos return to eastern Cuba. The "barrier" went from Mariel in the north coast of Cuba to Majana in the south shore. Since no supplies could enter by land, Maceo had to rely on the expeditions from Key West for weapons, ammunitions and new soldiers. Needles to say that Spain also intensified its naval presence in the area to intercept the supplies. Several times shipments from Key West saved Maceo's troops.

Maceo fought valiantly until December 7, 1886 when he was shot in an ambush in the San Pedro farm not far from Havana. Panchito Gomez Toro who was only in his twenties also died with Maceo. He refused to leave Maceo's body to be massacred by the Spanish troops and consequently met the same fate. Panchito was the son of Maximo Gomez. Maceo was his godfather. They both rest at a beautiful memorial in their honor near Havana.

The war continued bloody battle after bloody battle. Both sides experienced considerable human losses. By early 1898 the Cuban economy was practically paralyzed as the Mambises controlled most of the countryside.

But the Mambises did not have enough soldiers for a final push. It was a virtual stalemate. Maximo Gomez was facing an endless war.

Phillip II of Spain once said that "Whoever owns Cuba has the key to the New World". That idea was deeply rooted in Spain. During the wars in South America, the patriots under Bolivar and San Martin had faced no more than 70,000 Spanish troops. Spain had 400,000 armed soldiers in Cuba. This number included the Voluntarios. The Mambi Army never had more than 25,000 men. Many of them were not armed or had machetes only. Spain had to expend most of its troops protecting the cities , the main sugar mills and coffee , sugar plantations and other strategic sites.

Guerrilla tactics masterminded by Maximo Gomez, taking the Spanish army by surprise and the passion of a people seeking their freedom, exemplified by the courage of Antonio Maceo, made the difference. Maceo was the epitome of the fearless fighter. He was also a good strategist. He had over 28 bullet and sword wounds in his body by the time he died.

General Antonio Maceo died in battle on December 7, 1896.

IX

REMEMBER THE MAINE

The relationship between the United States and Spain during the second half of the 1800s was characterized by mutual distrust. The Navy contingency in Key West purposely would ignore the preparations and arms shipments that took place among the Cubans in the Keys. There is an anecdote of a U. S. Navy officer who went to talk to some of the Cubans in town and alerted them that he knew of the invasion that was being prepared and that he had orders not to let those ships depart. But he also offered advice; If you send the men alone to the island of Contoy, off the Mexican Caribbean coast, and you ship the arms in another boat, there is nothing that the Navy can do about it. Once everything is in Contoy then you can sail your army to Cuba, men and arms together. That is out of our jurisdiction.

Perhaps the best known expedition and that is because it transported quite a few of the old veterans and generals of the Ten Year War, was the one that left Key West on June 6th, 1895 to join the War for Cuba's Independence. The war had already started in February of that year. Among the best known participants of this saga were the Generals Serafin Sanchez and Carlos Roloff together with Colonel Rogelio Castillo and with Doctor Fermin Valdez Dominguez, among a few other high ranking officers. The beloved concierge of the San Carlos, Crescencio Cabrera was also part of the group. As inconspicuously as possible, all these Key West residents made their way over the sand dunes that were in the area where today you find Bertha Street and South Roosevelt Boulevard. Around this area they were picked up by a small boat that took them into an odyssey that lasted for two months. As a result of bad planning and bad luck, they were stuck, mostly hiding in Pine Key for nearly two months. There, they were eaten by mosquitoes, they were hungry and there were a few deserters. Finally on the 5th of July, General Mayia Rodriguez with another forty men picked them up in a large ship. On July 24th they landed in Punta Caney and were able to successfully unload all the weapons and all the military equipment. Soon they were fighting alongside the other insurgents. The news of the late but successful landing was received with much joy in Key West. The community needed some good news since they were still mourning the death of Jose Marti from two months earlier.

General Emilio Nuñez was responsible to coordinate expeditions to Cuba.

In January of 1898, the "Voluntarios" of Havana caused armed disturbances that put in jeopardy the lives of the American citizens and of the American embassy personnel in Havana. The U.S. government sent the U.S.S. Maine to Havana on a "good will tour." The Maine was based in Key West and it departed for Havana on January 24th. It anchored at Havana Bay. On February 15th a mysterious explosion destroyed it, leaving over two hundred and sixty navy personnel dead, and numerous wounded.

No other community in the U.S. suffered this loss as much as Key West did. These sailors only a month before were in the streets of Key West enjoying the year end celebrations. That night of February 15th there was an event going on in the San Carlos which was interrupted with the tragic news which had just been wired from Havana. The Maine had sunk in Havana bay with a tragic death toll. Quite a few of those sailors who died were well known in Key West. The Maine had one of the best baseball teams in the US Navy. Often during their visits to Key West they would play with other teams from the North Atlantic Squadron and with the excellent Key West local teams.

Monument to the victims of the USS Maine
in Key West cementery

Three days after the explosion, nineteen of the Maine victims were buried at the Colon cemetery in Havana. In the solemn procession there were more than 5,000 people walking behind the funerary march. Over 50,000 Havana residents viewed the procession in solemn respect. The houses in Havana all hung black ribbons and drapes from their balconies.

Many of the wounded were brought to Key West. Even the sisters converted the Convent of Mary Immaculate into a hospital. Eventually over a hundred and fifty of the victims were buried at the Colon cemetery in Havana. In December of 1899 they were all transferred to Arlington National Cemetery in Virginia. An American flag honors the twenty-seven sailors buried at the Maine Monument at our Key West cemetery. In 1954 the mayor of Havana, Justo Luis Pozo y del Puerto, presented a plaque in honor of the Maine victims. It can be seen at the entrance to the Maine monument in the Key West cemetery.

The USS Maine

This incident, and others, gave the United States government the reason or the excuse to declare war on Spain. Thus the War for Cuba's Independence became the Spanish-American War, The Spanish-American War lasted only four months, from April to August of 1898. The war was formally declared on April 25, 1898. Key West served as one of the key ports for the naval operations of this conflict. Over 150 American ships participated in the war. In early May the operations began with a Cuban naval blockade. A few naval skirmishes took place in the ports of Matanzas, Cardenas and Cienfuegos. Lieutenant General Calixto Garcia of the Mambi Army was contacted by letter by President McKinley. (See "A Message to Garcia" in the bonus chapter.) This letter set a meeting aboard the USS New York on June 3rd off the coast of Oriente Province. The main purpose was for the Mambi army to share logistics on the terrain and information about the Spanish troops. On June 10, 647 Marines landed at Guantanamo Bay. On June 22, 16,200 American soldiers under General Shafter's command landed at Daiquiri some 14 miles east of Santiago. The Mambi Army under General Demetrio Castillo Duany had secured the landing zone.

Mambises (Cuban insurgent army)
fought machete in hand.

General Garcia, Admiral Sampson and General Shafter met at El Aserradero to finalize strategies. The Mambi Army took the assignment to surround the Santiago regional area to prevent supplies and reinforcements and to prevent a Spanish retreat. The better armed and fed US Army would initially engage the Spanish troops. Spain could only deploy some 60,000 soldiers to the Santiago area. The remaining 340,000 men had to protect Havana and other major cities as well as the main sugar mills from the Mambi guerrilla tactics. On June 24th the first battle took place at Guasimas, east of Santiago. The following days the American troops kept successfully moving west. The battles of El Viso Fort, El Caney, San Juan Hill and others showed the American troops' superiority. The Gattling machine gun performed superbly. Future U.S. president Teddy Roosevelt and the Rough Riders rode into history.

Teddy Roosevelt lead the
Rough Riders to battle.

On July 3rd the Spanish fleet caught inside Santiago Bay tried to escape and is decimated by the American Navy waiting outside. At least a destroyer, a torpedo boat and four cruisers were sunk, 350 Spanish sailors died and 155 were wounded. Clara Barton and the American Red Cross took care of the wounded on all sides of the conflict. The Red Cross received high praises from all involved and from the international community.

General Calixto Garcia and 5,000 Mambises surrounded Santiago alongside the American troops. Santiago surrendered on July 17th. On August 12th the war ends. On December 10th. Spain and the US signed the formal Spanish surrender known as The Treaty of Paris. With the Treaty of Paris, Spain closes its colonial chapter in the Americas. As negotiated in the surrender, Spain gave the United States the colonies of Cuba, Puerto Rico, the Philippines, and Guam. In U.S. history the Spanish American War is known as the "Splendid Little War". We lost 385 soldiers and gained much international real estate and influence. For Spain the loss was devastating. A colonial power for over 400 years reaches its end. The psychological impact was deeper than the military and economic loss. Since then, there is a phrase commonly used in Spain up to these days "Mas se perdio en Cuba." "We lost more when we lost Cuba."

What a curious set of events for Key West. Since 1868 the Cuban community had been waging a war with Spain. Then suddenly after the Maine explosion the US government joins in the fight. The non Cuban residents of Key West all of a sudden join in the battle to see a free Cuba. The Key West community sees a carnival of warships. It is no longer a few brave local residents with a few Remingtons. It is the American Navy heading south to confront colonial Spain. What a feeling for this community.

It is curious how the Key West Cubans did not go back to Cuba immediately after the war. As far as they were concerned Cuba was not free yet. It was now under American occupation. The United States occupied Cuba until May 20th, 1902. On this day Cuba finally became a free republic. The community in Key West met at the San Carlos celebrating in unison with the festivities going on in Havana as the American flag was replaced by the Cuban flag over the Morro Fort.

A small exodus from Key West followed the establishment of the Cuban Republic. Given their bilingual skills, many Key West citizens obtained good paying jobs in the government and tourist industry. Many were hired by American companies that invested in Cuba. A neighborhood in Havana was named Cayo Hueso by some from here who settled there.

The dream of many for decades finally became a reality, a free Cuba. But to many Key West Cubans, to go back, was a difficult decision to make. Many had been in Key West since the 1860s. Children and grandchildren had been born in the Key. Key West was home. Many decided to stay. But for many of those who stayed, the mood dramatically changed in Key West. The Cuban community was accustomed to dedicate all their passion to the cause of a free Cuba. Now that Cuba was free there was sort of a vacuum. There was joy but, what do we do now ? Many in retrospection felt that the years as exiles were perhaps the best of possible times. A grandiose purpose, a struggle together as a community to reach a noble goal. Day after day striving to keep hope alive. All of a sudden Cuba is free and life becomes family, work, school, church , the normal. Where is La Banda Libertad, where is Poyo, Marti, the Yara newspaper? Why is the San Carlos so quiet? The legacy of a glorious era had taken over.

Many of today's citizens of Key West proudly descend from those who sacrificed so much for Cuba's liberty.

> *"I can't deliver from my heart, as I wanted to, all the tenderness, the just pride, the gratefulness that in the name of our country, we all owe to the Cuban immigrants of Key West."*
>
> *José Martí—In a letter to José D. Poyo, December 20, 1893*

X

AGUSTIN PARLA VS DOMINGO ROSILLO

Key West has contributed tremendously to the history of early aviation. Various chapters of great interest, all related to Cuba, took place here. One of these chapters was the competition between Domingo Rosillo and Agustin Parla to see who would be the first to fly an airplane between Key West and Havana.

Domingo Rosillo del Toro was born in Algeria in October of 1878 of Spanish parents. He mostly lived in Spain and studied aviation in Paris, graduating as a certified pilot in 1912. He moved to Cuba for the purpose of becoming the first pilot to cross the Straits of Florida.

Agustin Parla Orduna was born in Key West on October 10, 1887. His father, a Cuban immigrant, owned a toy store in Key West and was a good friend of Jose Marti. The store was located near South Beach. Agustin moved to Cuba at age six. He was the first Cuban known to have piloted a plane when a friend, who was a teacher at the Curtis School of Aviation, took him along for a ride over Havana and let him fly the plane. At an early age, and with great financial sacrifices he enrolled in the Curtis School of Aviation in Miami and graduated in 1912. He was the first Cuban to be certified as an airplane pilot.

In 1912 the City of Havana and the Curtis School of Aviation announced a competition to find the first pilot to cover the 110 miles between Key West and Havana. The main purpose was to promote the aviation industry and to include Cuba among the pioneers of the industry.

Both Rosillo and Parla signed up for the challenge. Rosillo went to Key West where he waited for the arrival of his plane, a single Gnome engine French made Morane-Saulnier. Parla, through friends and family, financed a Curtis hydroplane with an 80 horsepower engine. Both pilots had much support from the public. In Key West Parla was favored, being a local son.

On March 17, 1913 both pilots were ready to depart. The US Navy ships "Peoria" and "Yamalkraw" would keep an eye on the planes for the first 25 miles over the ocean. All three ships of the Cuban Navy were also assigned positions along the route. The "Patria" was placed 45 miles from Havana. The "Hatuey" was at 30 miles and the "24 de Febrero" at 15 miles. La Punta park, across from the Morro Castle, at the entrance to Havana Bay was packed with people waiting for the cannon shot which would signal the departure from Key West.

Agustin Parla, born in Key West became the first director of Cuba's aviation.

The weather that day was a little windy. Rosillo departed around 5:10 A.M. It was not easy for him to stabilize his "motorized kite" as some had nicknamed his plane. But finally he was able to control it and head south. Parla, with much difficulty, was able to depart over the rough waves of South Beach at 5:57 AM. But he had to return immediately due to mechanical failure.

After 2 hours, 30 minutes and 40 seconds of flying, Domingo Rosillo lands in Havana at the Columbia army barracks. Being the first one to arrive, he receives the $10,000 price. The celebrations in Havana reached carnival proportions.

Back in Key West, Agustin Parla quietly fixes his hydroplane. Without telling anyone, on the morning of May 19th he takes off for Havana. There were no ships in the ocean to assist him and only a compass to guide him. Inside the hydroplane he carried a Cuban flag that Jose Marti had often flown at events in Key West. One of his relatives sent a message to Havana informing the authorities. When people in Havana heard the news, they went to the Malecon street bordering the coast looking up for Parla. But Parla barely avoided a crash landing at San Lazaro Cove inside Mariel Bay a few miles from Havana. Many who saw him went to help him come ashore. Another carnival like party ensued when the news that Parla had landed at Mariel reached Havana. He was given the second prize award of $5,000.

A few years later Agustin Parla was appointed the director of Cuba's civil aviation. He served a brilliant career and helped develop Cuba's aviation in many ways. One particularly interesting chapter in his career was when General Jose Marti, son of the "Cuban Apostle of Independence" and a top General in the Cuban Army, sent Parla to Buffalo, New York to visit Curtis School of Aviation headquarters to explore if Curtis could set up in Havana a school to train the Cuban air forces.

Parla died on July 31, 1946. A bust in his honor can be seen at Key West airport on the second floor departures lounge. His passion for flying was key in the successful development of Cuba's aviation.

Domingo Rosillo went to teach aviation in Barcelona for many years. Later in life he returned to Havana where he died in 1957.

On the walls of the second floor cafeteria at the Key West airport departures lounge you can see numerous pictures, drawings, and newspaper clippings on this wonderful, early aviation chapter.

This cover flew in Aeromarine Key West to Havana first flight
on November 1st, 1920.

This cover flew in Pan American Key West to Havana
first fly on October 19th, 1927.

XI

AEROMARINE & PAN AMERICAN

The following early aviation historical chapter also took place in Key West. In 1920 Florida West Indies Airways won the contract to carry the USA mail from Key West to Havana. But due to lack of funding, it was not going to be able to comply with the contract. Aeromarine Plane and Motor Company of New Jersey created Aeromarine West Indies Airways and bought the contract from FWIA and thus became the first airline to carry air mail between Key West and Havana.

AWIA bought six Curtis F-5-L hydroplanes from the U.S. Navy and converted them into luxurious passenger crafts. These hydroplanes would carry passengers as well as the mail between Key West and Havana. On November 1, 1920 the "La Pinta" and the "Santa Maria" hydroplanes of AWIA initiated the historical first passenger and air mail flight between Key West and Havana. These crafts were equipped with two Liberty engines of 400 horsepower each. They could carry 9 passengers in two luxurious mahogany cabins with individual leather seats. Each seat was next to a window so that the passenger could enjoy the view. They would fly at an average altitude of 30 feet above sea level. The trip lasted around 85 minutes. The crew was made up of three, a pilot, a copilot and a mechanic who doubled as a passenger assistant. Each passenger could carry 30 pounds of luggage.

AWIA was very successful in the first years of this venture. It was able to expand these services to other Caribbean islands. During its first year of operation it carried over 2,000 passengers between Key West and Havana. These daily flights were scheduled to coincide with the arrival of the train from Miami to Key West. But in 1923 a tragic accident seemed to have changed its luck. Only 20 miles away from reaching Havana a mechanical failure force the plane into an abrupt ocean landing. Four passengers died. Soon after AWIA collapsed.

In 1927 Pan American Airways is created, sheltered by a contract with the U.S. Postal Service to carry the mail between Key West and Havana. This contract required that by October 19th the first sack of American mail had to be in Havana. Pan American had purchased various Fokker F-7 tri motors for this service. But unusual heavy rains had fallen over Key West and the Fokkers could not take off from Meacham Field due to the heavy mud. Luckily one of the old AWIA hydroplanes was in Key West and Pan Am was able to rent it to comply with the first day of the contract on October 19, 1927. Nine days later, on October 28, Pan Am began the first scheduled international airmail route in the world from Havana to Key West and back. Three months later, on January 10, 1928 the scheduled passenger flights also began. Thus one of the most loved and missed airlines of the world, was born in Key West.

The first office of Pan American Airways was located at La Concha Hotel in Key West. Soon after, they moved to the corner of Whitehead and Caroline streets where Kelly's Restaurant is nowadays. On the side of the building over Caroline there is a plaque commemorating this historical location.

This sign appears at today's Kelly's Restaurant celebrating Pan American Airways birthplace in Key West.

THE AIR-WAY TO HAVANA

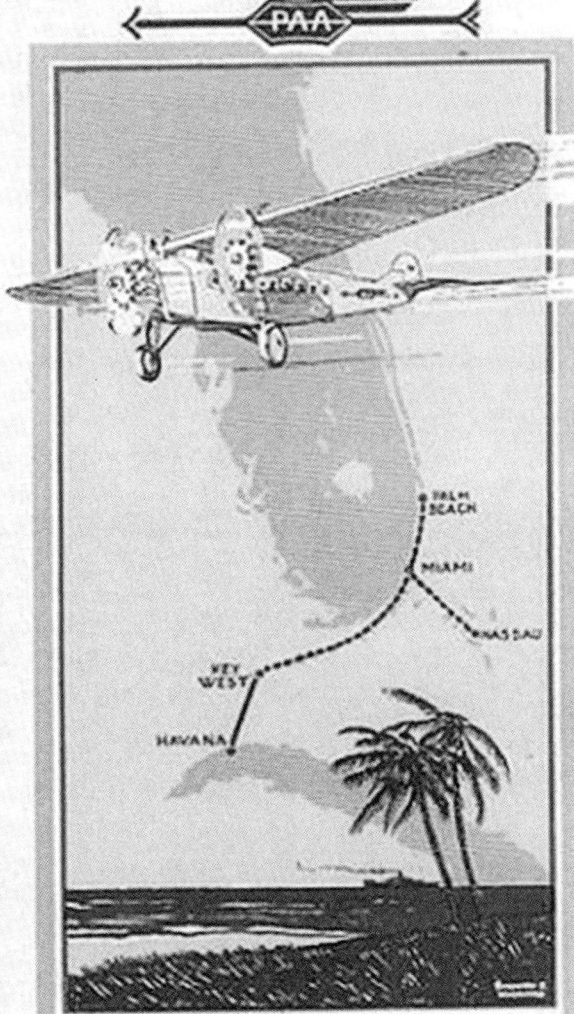

PAA

PALM BEACH
MIAMI
NASSAU
KEY WEST
HAVANA

PAN AMERICAN AIRWAYS, INC.
PERSHING SQUARE BUILDING
NEW YORK

XII

RELATED NOTES

Xerez and Torres discover Taino Indian smoking rolled tobacco leaves in Cuba in 1492.

EARLY TOBACCO BRIEFS

I have always been at odds with the thought that civilization came from Europe. The Tainos who inhabited Cuba gave modern languages three words that attest to the contrary; hammock, barbecue and tobacco.

The first time a European came in contact with tobacco smoking was in 1492 during Columbus' first voyage. When Columbus landed in Cuba he sent a group to explore the coast. Leading this group were Rodrigo de Xerez and Luis Torres. They came across a village where they saw a native "taking in smoke from dry leaves wrapped like a musket."

One of the greatest tobacco promoters of all time was Jean Nicot. He was the French ambassador to Portugal between 1559 and 1561. He became very interested in everything coming in from the New World. He would keep an eye for vessels coming into Lisbon from the Americas in order to observe first hand the curious cargo. He became fascinated with sniffing and smoking tobacco leaves. He spread the practice throughout Europe, especially among the French aristocracy. Now you know where the word nicotine comes from.

Jean Nicot, French ambassador to Portugal was fascinated by the tobacco leaves.

THE LOYALTY OF FREEMASONS

My father was a very active Freemason in Cuba. When he came to the United States, he stopped participating. Starting life at point 0 at 53 years of age in a foreign country was too complicated. Once or twice I asked him what went on inside the Masonic Lodges which was so secret. He sort of avoided my question every time I asked. The loyalty of Freemasons to secrecy and to each other has always drawn my curiosity. In researching this book I came across a Key West story that I think you will enjoy.

The Spanish consuls of Key West had a tough job. They were supposed to spy on the community and report to Havana. They were hated and subjected to abuse by the local Cubans. Many times the Spanish flag was stolen or burnt from the front of the consulate. When walking the streets the consul and the mission employees would be subjected to weaseling and other harassments. But one of the consuls was able to cross the line into acceptance and that is because he was a Freemason active in the Felix Varela Lodge. His name was Pedro Solis.

A Mexican army general named Catarino Erasmo de la Garza had revolted against the corrupt government of Porfirio Diaz in Mexico and was persecuted by that government. Seeking refuge in the United States, he found out that because of an extradition agreement with Mexico, the U.S. government was also after him. He was able to escape to Nassau and eventually made his way to Key West. He wanted to help the Cubans with their war and he knew the Cubans were no fans of Diaz. Somehow he appeared at the Monroe Hotel, at the corner of Truman and Whitehead, owned by Martin Herrera. At the hotel, Garza and Herrera became friends. Garza was from a very wealthy Mexican family and received plenty of money from them. He was a charming well-educated man of fine manners and also a Freemason. He felt very comfortable among the Cubans in Key West to the point that he told a few his true story. Soon the whole town knew that a fugitive of Mexico and the U.S. was living at the Monroe. The word also reached the Spanish consul, Pedro Solis. Solis alerts the authorities who alert Herrera that a fugitive lives in his hotel. Being a Freemason himself Herrera seeks fellow Freemason Gerardo

Castellanos' help. Castellanos hides Garza in the second floor of his house, 521 Truman, for quite a few months. Mexican and federal agents seek the fugitive in Key West. Both governments were offering high bounties for Garzas' head.

Castellanos has to leave Key West indefinitely on a Jose Marti mission to Cuba. But before he leaves he has to find a way to help Garza escape. His less risky option was to trust his Masonic brother, Pedro Solis, the Spanish consul.

Castellanos and Solis met. Solis meets Garza and agrees to help him out.

They actually found much in common. They were both highly educated from wealthy families, well-traveled and Freemasons and both hated Porfirio Diaz.

Solis, in his position as Spanish consul, convinced the local authorities that Garza has left town in a steamer bound for Philadelphia and New York. Eventually Garza left for Costa Rica via Havana, disguised as a Spanish citizen, accompanied by Solis.

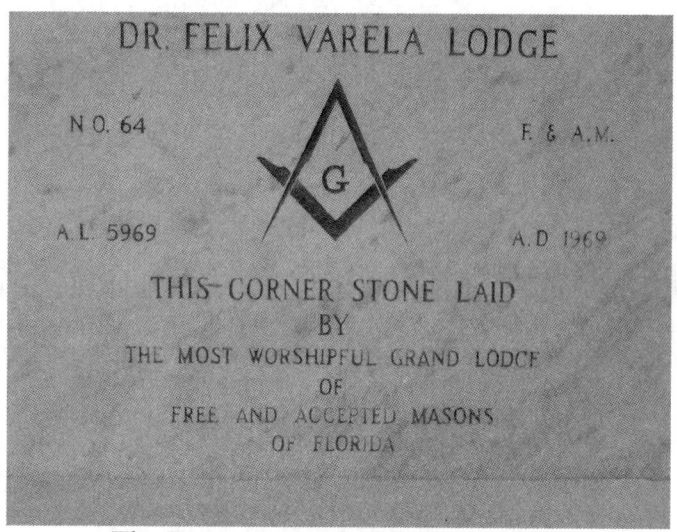

The Freemasons played a key role in Cuba's Independence.

A MESSAGE TO GARCIA

On April 24, 1898 President McKinley had called Colonel Arthur Wagner in charge of the U.S. Bureau of Military Intelligence to an urgent meeting.

The next day the war with Spain would be officially declared and he needed to send an urgent letter to Lieutenant General Calixto Garcia of the Cuban insurgent army. But Garcia was deep in the mountains of eastern Cuba leading the guerrilla war against Spain. No one knew exactly where he was and there was no mail nor telegraph service. But the letter needed to reach him as soon as possible. The success of the war was depending on its delivery.

General Calixto Garcia Iñiguez

Colonel Wagner told the President that if anyone could deliver the letter, it was Lieutenant Andrew S. Rowan. The President asked how. Colonel Wagner responded that he had no idea how, but he knew Rowan could do it.

On May 1st. Rowan handed the letter to Garcia deep in the Cuban mountains.

He returns with a message for McKinley. On June 3rd the Mambises (Cuban insurgent army) and the U.S. Marines meet aboard the USS New York somewhere off the coast of eastern Cuba to plan the war. Rowan who was 32 years old at the time was promoted to captain.

In 1899 a journalist by the name of Elbert Hubbard wrote an essay entitled "A Message to Garcia". He used the story above as a motivational example as to how self confidence, positivism and perseverance can take you far. No one knows how Rowan got to Garcia. But he did.

The essay was a tremendous success and was published repeatedly in many text books during the 1930s, 1940s and 1950s. "A Message to Garcia" became a synonym with "Yes, you can do it."

JUANA BORRERO, GLORIA DE CUBA

Esteban Borrero was a well-known medical doctor and poet during the late 19th. century. He lived with his family in a wealthy neighborhood in the outskirts of Havana bordering the Almendares River. His wife and all four children were also very talented painters, poets and musicians. In particular, one of the older girls, Juana, distinguished herself since a very early age as a painter and poet.

Juana was born on May 18, 1877 in Havana. Her paintings and poems were so outstanding at such a young age that her father used to give them as gifts to friends in the literary circles of Havana. At age fifteen she was accepted into the prestigious San Alejandro School of Arts. Already her poems and paintings had graced the top literary magazines in Havana. During a visit to New York in 1894 she gave Jose Marti a painting of a palm tree to "tropicalize" his apartment in that city. She was only 17 years old. Her early maturity was seasoned by the War for Cuba's Independence which began in early 1895.

Juana Borrero maintained a secret and tormented relationship with Carlos Pio Urbach. This relation was against her father's wishes. Carlos was a student at the University of Havana and belonged to its intellectual elite. He edited several literary magazines and newspapers in Havana. On a daily basis they would write to each other. Through an elaborate network of friends the letters were secretly delivered. They got to see each other very little. This tormented relationship led Juana to passionate poetry and also inspired her paintings.

Juana was not feeling very well in January of 1896. But she hid from her family her discomforts. That same month revolutionary activities against the Spanish colonial rule of Cuba placed her father in a difficult and dangerous path. The decision was made to emigrate to Key West immediately. To leave Carlos behind added to Juana's suffering.

The Borrero family travelled to Key West aboard the Olivetti in late January. The first few days they stayed at the Hotel Duval. Soon they rented an apartment on Duval Street upstairs from Day Allen & Company, a furniture store. Esteban was hired by the San Carlos Institute as an instructor.

Juana was miserable in Key West. Her worsening health, lack of letters and distance from Carlos constantly afflicted her entire being. From her apartment window she could see the ocean and looked for ships that could bring Carlos' letters. Due to her increasing discomforts on most days she only ventured to the post office , sometimes to the cemetery and also to the San Carlos where she listened to her father's lectures. Aside from her sisters her only friend was a young nun. At home she spent much of her time painting happy pieces for the children at the convent.

Juana Borrero "Gloria de Cuba" rests in the Key West cemetery

Carlos was supposed to come visit Key West. But several responsibilities kept delaying his visit. Juana kept writing to him on a daily basis and with each letter her ill health became more apparent. The Borreros finally found out that she was suffering from typhoid fever. Both Cuba and Key West were subjected to a large deadly epidemic. Juana died on March 9, 1896 only seven weeks after leaving

Cuba and Carlos behind. He never made it to Key West to see Juana for a last time.

Juana's death totally afflicted Carlos' life. He came to Key West a few weeks after her death. Most of the time he would be found crying by her tomb. After a month or so in Key West he returned to Cuba. He joined the War against Spain under the command of General Jose Maria Aguirre. He was assigned as one of Aguirres' top aids. He soon rose to the rank of Lieutenant Coronel in the Mambi Army. He died in the fields of Matanzas on December 17, 1897. He was 25 years old.

When Cuba became a free Republic in 1902, the Borrero family returned to Cuba. Juana's remains stayed at the Key West cemetery. It is not clear how it happened, but her remains were lost for a while. It seems she was at rest at a tomb belonging to members of the Felix Valera Lodge. But somehow in 1973 a generous Rivera family put her to rest in her own grave, where she currently rests, very near the monument to the Maine victims here in our Key West Cemetery.

The history of Juana's and Carlos' love is alive thanks to a wonderful book written in Cuba in 1984 and printed in Madrid by Belkis Cuza Male, entitled "El Clavel y la Rosa". Belkis is currently a contributor to the Miami Herald en Espanol and also the owner and chief editor of the prestigious Linden Lane Magazine.

Every May 18th at noon, a few Key West citizens visit her tomb remembering this young talented life who stayed behind alone.

The Mercedes Hospital building can be seen at 1209 Virginia Street in Key West

HOSPITAL LAS MERCEDES

In 1910 a group of Cuban ladies from Key West started a hospital to take medical care of the poor in the city.

The always humanitarian tobacco baron Eduardo Hidalgo Gato donated his old mansion for this purpose. The mansion was moved from its original location at Bay View Park to its current location on Virginia Street. The hospital received its name in honor of Gato's wife, Mercedes, who was one of its leading ladies. It had 5 rooms with 28 beds.

Dr. Fogarty, who had been a Key West mayor, was the first medical director. But the person who tirelessly cared for the hospital and its patients was Maria V. de Gutsens. In 1934 she received the highest award given by the Cuban government, the "Orden de Carlos Manuel de Cespedes", recognizing her many years of devotion to this noble cause. For many years the poor of Key West received excellent free medical care in its quarters.

Do not miss this beautiful building at 1209 Virginia Street near White.

The historical house where Cuban consul Carrasco lived
in the corner of Eaton and Grinnell Streets in Key West.

ANTONIO DIAZ Y CARRASCO

Key West had the largest concentration of Cubans in the U.S. followed by Tampa and New York City when Cuba became a republic. The new Cuban government, soon after its establishment, sent Antonio Diaz y Carrasco as Cuban consul to Key West.

Carrasco was born in the Key and had studied at the San Carlos. He knew the city and the community very well. The first Cuban consulate building was in the corner of Eaton and Grinnell. The historical house is still standing. Often Carrasco would address the crowds from the beautiful second floor semi circular balcony which still can be seen in that corner. He died in 1915. Carrasco rests in the Cuban Ten Year War Memorial in the Key West cemetery. He is the only person buried in that plot.

BIBLIOGRAPHY

Alpizar Poyo, Raoul: *Cayo Hueso y Jose Dolores Poyo, Dos Simbolos Patrios*, Imp. P. Fernandez y Cia., La Habana 1947.
Autor Desconocido, panfleto, City of Key West, *Huella de Herencia Cubana*. Instituto San Carlos.
Byrne, Ricardo A.: *Apuntes Sobre la Historia de la Masoneria Cubana*, Imprenta del Sol XX, La Habana 1913.
Figueredo Socarras, Fernando: *Conferencia: Jose Dolores Poyo*, Ofrecida por el autor V.M. De la R. Logia Cuba ante la velada funebre que a su recuerdo dedicara dicha Logia. Imp. P. Fernandez y Comp. LaHabana, 1912.
Figueredo Socarras, Fernando: *La Revolucion de Yara 1868-1878*, M. Pulico y Compania, Amargura 30, La Habana 1902.
Garcia Pascual, Luis: *Destinatario – Jose Marti*, Casa Editora Abril, La Habana Cuba, 2005-
Garcia, Rafael: *El Correo Aereo en Cuba, Primeros Vuelos*, Club Filatelico de la Republica de Cuba, La Habana 1937.
Castellanos G, Gerardo: *Motivos de Cayo Hueso*, Ucar, Garcia y Cia. La Habana, Cuba, 1935.
Castellanos G. Gerardo: *Mision a Cuba, Cayo Hueso y Marti*, Ucar, Garcia y Cia, La Habana Cuba 1944.
Chaffin, Tom: *Fatal Glory, Narciso Lopez and the First Clandestine U.S. War Against Cuba*. University Press of Virgina, Charlottesville 1996.
Costa, Octavio R.: *Antonio Maceo El Heroe*, Editora Corripio C. Por A. Santo Domingo 1950.
Deulofeu Lleonart, Manuel: *Marti, Cayo Hueso y Tampa; La Emigracion, Notas Historicas*, Cienfuegos, Cuba 1905.
Guerra Aguiar, J. L.: *Historia Postal de Cuba, Museo Postal Cubano* 1985.
Hambright, Tom: *Key West and Cuba become Link for International Communications*. International Ocean Telegraph Company in Key West. *Florida Key Sea Heritage Journal*, Fall 1999.
Maloney, Walter C.: *A Sketch of the History of Key West, Florida 1876*. A Facsimile Reproduction, University of Florida Press Gainesville, Florida 1968.

Manach, Jorge: *Marti, El Apostol*, Coleccion Austral, Espasa-Calpe S.A., Madrid 1942.

Martinez, Cristobal: *Notas Sobre el Correo Aereo en Cuba*, The Cuban
Philatelist, Vol XXI No. 58, Enero-Abril 2010.

Martinez-Fernandez, Luis: *Protestantism and Political Conflict in the Nineteenth-Century Hispanic Caribbean*, Rutgers University Press, New Brunswick, New Jersey ,2002.

Perez, Louis A.: *Jose Marti in the United States*: The Florida Experience, ASU Center for Latin American Studies, Arizona State University, Tempe, 1995.

Poyo, Gerald E.: *Key West and the Cuban Ten Years War*, The Florida Historical Quaterly Vol.57 No. 3 , January 1979.

Quesada y Miranda, Gonzalo de: *Marti, Hombre*, Editorial Cubana, Miami 1998.

Ronning, C. Neale: *Jose Marti and the Émigré Colony in Key West*, Praeger Publishers, New York, NY 1990.

Stebbins, Consuelo E.: *City of Intrigue, Nest of Revolution, A Documentary. History of Key West in the Nineteeth Century*, University Press of Florida, 2007.

U.S. Postal Commemorative Society, *The First International Passenger Service Key West to Havana*, a brochure.

Westfall, Dr. Loy Glenn: *Key West Cigar City USA*, Book One of Floridas Cigar City Triology, 1997.

USEFUL KEY WEST WEB SITES

Key West Chamber of Commerce	—	www.keywestchamber.org
San Carlos Institute	—	www.institutosancarlos.org
Key West Literary Seminar	—	www.kwls.org
Art & History Museum	—	www.kwahs.com
Key West Cuban American Heritage	—	www.cubanfest.com
Paintings & Intaglios	—	www.keywestfolkart.com
Butterfly Conservatory	—	www.keywestbutterfly.com
Cuban food and Music	—	www.elmesondepepe.com
Florida Keys Music	—	www.milemarker24.com
Water sports	—	www.furycat.com
Cuban Stamps	—	www.ilastamps.com
Cuban Food and Art	—	www.havana1keywest.webs.com
Cuban Art	—	www.cubaenmi.blogspot.com
Cuban Art	—	www.sandyrico-81.wix.com/artwork
Cuban Art	—	www.abelquintero.com

**Havana 1 Restaurant
Key West
(305) 294-5050**

HAVANA 1,
CUBAN RESTAURANT
AND ART GALLERY
1101 TRUMAN, KEY WEST.

DELICIOUS CUBAN

CUISINE

IN KEY WEST

(Art by Juan Ego)

Juan loves Lucy
Restaurant
Duval St., Key West